Built upon the Cornerstone

Built upon the Cornerstone

A Brief History of the Christian Church

by

Joseph M. Tewinkel

Christian Publications, Inc.

Christian Publications, Inc.
25 S. 10th Street, P.O. Box 3404
Harrisburg, PA 17105

The mark of ❡ *vibrant faith*

Cover Photo: The Cathedral at Worms

Library of Congress Catalog Card Number 80-65148
© 1980 by Christian Publications, Inc. All rights reserved
ISBN 0-87509-280-2
Printed in the United States of America

Contents

Introduction   7

1   Building on Strong Foundations   10

2   Building through Storm and Test   20

3   Building under Government Pressure   31

4   Building When the Culture Collapses   41

5   Building in Dark Days   51

6   Building through Reform   65

7   Building with Reforming Zeal   75

8   Building in War and Opposition   87

9   Building in Revival   98

10   Building in a New Land   109

11 Building on the Frontier   119

12 Building in the Modern Age   131

13 Building to the Ends of the Earth   143

   Glossary   161

   Bibliography   175

Introduction

The criticisms and accusations come from all sides: "The church is weak." "It is irrelevant to the needs of modern society." "It is fractured into many groups." "It is divided in its witness." "It is powerless and unspiritual." The young person demonstrating for a cause, the advocate of church renewal, and the concerned pastor—all join in decrying the weakness of the twentieth century church.

But the picture such people draw is incomplete. For all its weaknesses and faults, the church is God's institution. Jesus had asked His disciples who men said He was. Turning to Peter, He then asked who Peter said He was. Upon Peter's glorious confession of Jesus as the Christ, the Son of the living God, Jesus declared that upon this foundation He would build His church and that the gates of hell should not prevail against it (Matt. 16:18).

The church is not insignificant or irrelevent. It is the building of Christ Himself. Paul expands this concept. "And are built upon the foundation of the apostles and prophets, Jesus Christ himself being the chief corner stone; In whom all the building fitly framed together groweth unto an holy temple in the Lord: In whom ye also are builded together for an habitation of God through the Spirit" (Eph. 2:22 KJV).

Christ is the cornerstone upon which both the foundation and the building are constructed. He is head over all things to the Church. The Church stands sure and triumphant upon the Cornerstone—Christ Jesus.

A study of church history is one of the best ways to realize the truth of God's activity in building His church. We often view events and situations through the narrow perspective of our own experience. But history shows us the broad picture. In spite of seeming defeat, the sinfulness of man, heresy within, and persecution without, Jesus Christ continues to build His church. The gates of hell, though strongly menacing throughout the ages, have not prevailed against it.

Church history can be an exciting study—of real people and their struggles and victories. The record must always be a true one, however. We shall attempt to be accurate even where truth does not come out as we wish it would. We shall not gloss over the problems or errors of the past.

An understanding of the past can help us find our "roots." Evangelicals have typically thought of themselves as having little dependence upon the past beyond the New Testament era. But the twenty centuries in between have indeed shaped the church today. We do have a past, even if we have not always admitted it!

The numerous religious groups on the scene today become comprehensible to the student of church history. He is more understanding and therefore less irresponsibly bigoted.

Church history can assist us to avoid the repetition of the

errors of the past. As Solomon said, "There is nothing new under the sun." Old heresies in new garb frequently occur. Positively, our heritage can be a stimulus to faith and devotion to Christ. Great men of God of the past challenge us to follow in their train. Not just the ancient apostles, but more recent servants of the Savior have also "turned the world upside down" for Christ. What God has done before, He can and will do again. He has built, is building, and will continue to build His church.

1

Building on Strong Foundations

Time line   0   100   200   300 400 500 600

A solid foundation is imperative to the construction of any building which is to last. The church, the body of Christ, has been built upon an unshakeable base. Christ Himself, of course, provides the ultimate source and beginning of His church (Acts 3:11).

Preparation of the World for the Gospel

God did not operate carelessly in other aspects of the inauguration of the Christian era. The setting for the initiation of the church was carefully prepared. Paul, in Galatians 4:4, said, "But when the time had fully come, God sent forth His Son." Varied cultural elements had shaped the ancient world. God superintended that process, creating an optimum situation for the early church to be born, to develop, and to grow.

The Empire of Rome dominated the Mediterranean world in the early centuries of Christian history. While Rome later was to prove a formidable foe of the Gospel, the early Christian message was expedited through Rome-provided vehicles. One central government meant peace and stability to the Mediterranean world. It provided good roads and improved modes of transportation. The Roman army was everywhere, maintaining order. The "pax Romana," or Roman peace, made possible missionary travel and preaching in widespread areas. While numerous exceptions eventually occurred, Roman rule allowed considerable local diversity in custom and religion, permitting Christianity to develop. Law, not the whim of a ruler, was the basis of society. In comparison with some earlier empires, Rome was actually quite tolerant.

Greek culture pervaded the eastern Mediterranean. From the time of Alexander the Great in the 300s B.C., the Greek language had been the dominant literary vehicle. Communication among nations was therefore simplified. It is no accident that the New Testament was written originally in Koine, or common, Greek. Greek culture also provided a depth of philosophical inquiry unknown elsewhere. While the philosophers surely were not Christians, the kinds of questions they asked dissipated the superstitious belief in many gods. The bankruptcy of the old Greco-Roman gods was revealed. It was no longer intellectually respectable to believe the traditional myths. The new curiosity of the Greek philosophers may have awakened a sense of searching and need.

The Scriptures clearly teach that the times were "full" for Christ's coming because of God's past dealings with Israel. Theological ideas basic to Christianity were long a part of Jewish life — sin, sacrifice, monotheism, a personal God, revelation, and forgiveness. Some in Israel were earnestly looking for a Messiah. The Old Testament itself was a vital preparation for the church. Jewish religious life in the synagogue system had been dispersed through much of the Roman Empire and Gentiles increasingly became proselytes. According to the Book of Acts, many of the first converts to Christianity were Gentile proselytes.

Thus the world was prepared for the dramatic invasion of God in human flesh—the person of Jesus Christ.

The New Testament

The life and ministry of Jesus is history. It must never be forgotten that our faith is based upon historical fact—Jesus was born, lived, taught, performed miracles, died on a cross, and rose from the dead. Our faith is not based upon myth or fable.

The glorious outpouring of the Holy Spirit at Pentecost must surely be recognized as foundational to the building of the church. Exciting as the experiences of that day were, they were only a beginning. Empowered by the Spirit, the Christians told the good news in Jerusalem, Judea, Samaria, and to the ends of their world. The Book of Acts provides the first church history book. We learn of the inclusion of the first Gentile converts, the warmth of early fellowship and Christian sharing, early missionary trips, apostolic preaching methods, fledgling church organization, persecution, miracles, expanding leadership, and new regions opened to the Gospel.

The conversion of Saul of Tarsus was a high point of early church life in that this man became the outstanding spokesman for the Christian community. His letters, along with the writings of other apostolic figures, provide the church with its basic theological position.

This study does not include a detailed treatment of the New Testament church. It is assumed that persons using this material already will have a familiarity with that exciting story. It is our purpose to emphasize the post-apostolic ages. In no way, however, should the reader conclude that the New Testament is insignificant to church history. On the contrary, it is of utmost importance in understanding later events.

Expansion

Jesus had given direct instructions to His disciples to spread the message of the Gospel throughout the world. The Book of Acts witnesses the beginnings of the fulfillment of Christ's "marching orders." The expansion of the church has continued ever since. By the twentieth century, Christianity has become the most widespread of all faiths. How effectively did the church spread the Gospel in the first three centuries?

By the year 100, the church was strongly represented in Syria, Asia Minor (modern Turkey), Macedonia and Achaia (modern Greece), and Rome. Asia Minor was probably the most thoroughly Christian area. In the following 200 years the Gospel entered new lands and more completely penetrated previously evangelized regions.

The birthplace of Christianity, the eastern Mediterranean, saw uneven acceptance of its message. The Jews were slow to accept Jesus as Messiah, so Palestine proper had a relatively small church. Syria, however, with its principal city Antioch, was a stronghold of the faith. By the early 300s, records show twenty bishops in that area; therefore numerous groups of Christians must have been in existence.

Asia Minor continued to witness great growth. This fortunate state developed because of the disintegration of the old religions, Paul's effective ministry there earlier, and the strong Greek cultural influences of the area.

Tradition says that Mark was an early preacher of the

good news in Egypt. The Gospel became widely accepted both by the Greek-speaking populations of the coast and the native peoples up the Nile river. Carthage, the great city of North Africa (the modern Tunisia area), soon heard the message, perhaps from traders or merchants. Eventually Carthage became a key center of Latin-speaking Christianity.

We don't know when the Gospel first arrived in Rome. We do know from Acts 28 that Christians were there when Paul first arrived. Possibly, according to an ancient tradition, both Peter and Paul had a share in discipling believers in the imperial capital. The church grew in the city itself, reaching several thousand in number by the year 300, and expanded to other parts of Italy.

The western Mediterranean area, also, was reached early. Christians from Asia Minor went to Gaul (modern France). Merchants and business people helped establish strong churches in the cities. By the 300s, records show twenty-five bishops in Gaul. Even Spain, the site of Paul's long-desired ministry, heard the Gospel in the early years, although there are records indicating serious problems in the church there. Tertullian, writing about 200, mentions Christians in Britain, far to the northwest. Again, most likely traders and businessmen first took the Gospel to that land, although converted Roman soldiers stationed there may have shared in that privilege.

Christians also witnessed east of Jerusalem, beyond the bounds of the Roman Empire. By crossing political frontiers, the Christian faith demonstrated that it was for the human race, not just the Romans. By 300, many believers were found in Mesopotamia (modern Iraq). They had a well-organized church and a flourishing school. Large portions of the Bible were available to them.

Tradition says that the Apostle Thomas began the

church in India. Surely the ancient Mar Thoma church attests to its early establishment. The writer Eusebius, about 180, tells of a visit to India of a man from Alexandria who found Christians already there. In Armenia (on the borders of Iran, Turkey, and the U.S.S.R. today) the ruler, King Triadates, became a Christian about 300, the first recorded Christian head of state.

While faithful men sowed and watered the seed, God gave the increase of harvest growth. The Holy Spirit was effectually at work through the church, bringing men and women to Himself. But the early Christians apparently utilized sound strategies to increase their effectiveness. The ancient world was an urban world, much like the world of the twentieth century. Evidence suggests that the church was planted in the great cities first and from them moved to the surrounding countryside. Laymen were active in telling the story of Christ. Undoubtedly people who would be termed "professional missionaries" today participated. However, no records exist of such persons from the time of Paul in the first century to that of Ulfilas in the fourth. Laymen carried a major share of the spreading of the Gospel.

We cannot be sure of the exact number of Christians because modern poll-taking and census practices were not used. Possibly between 5 and 14 percent of the population of the Roman Empire was Christian by the year 300. The Christians were a signifiant minority, increasing each year. Christ indeed was building His church!

Church Life

What was it like to be a Christian in the first three centuries? Would a twentieth century American Christian feel at home in the church? Although cultures have changed, common interests, practices, and attitudes which we see today were present then. Perhaps the church then might have been more compatible to us than one might think.

Attending corporate worship on Sundays was very important to early Christians. They read the Old Testament and such portions of the New Testament letters as were available. Leaders expounded these and exhorted believers to Christian living. Singing, corporate prayer, collections, and distribution to the needy also were a part of the service.

The two New Testament ordinances were featured prominently in early church life. Baptism was a significant testimony to the surrounding world that one was a believer. New Christians fasted prior to being baptized, according to the *Didache,* an ancient record of the period. The Lord's Supper, too, was an important part of regular church practice. At first it was observed together with the love feast, a common meal. Later the two were separated. Often the meetings of the church were divided between the reading and preaching segment, open to all, and the Lord's Supper, which was attended only by baptized believers.

In the first two centuries, the high moral standards of the Christian community were widely known and stood out in sharp contrast with the looseness of pagan society. Galen, a second century physician, described Christians in their self-discipline and morality as being "not a whit behind real philosophers." For that culture, it was a high compliment.

We must not, of course, put halos of inaccurate description around the early church. Problems existed then too—even in the first century, as the Corinthian letter illustrates. Sometimes the problem of the second generation caused difficulty. The children of believers, if they too had not personally acknowledged Christ, were cast into limbo. They were not real Christians, yet were regarded as such by the pagan community. Evidence suggests a problem, too, with group conversions in the third century with resulting increased worldiness. Christians denounced the carnage of the Roman gladiatorial games. Generally Christians in these centuries opposed the warfare which was so common in the period. Many were pacifists.

Love and concern for one another and the needy were badges worn by the early church. The New Testament practice of caring for widows was extended and expanded. In Alexandria in the 250s, Christians distinguished themselves caring for the sick in a plague which swept the city. Slaves were readily and freely accepted as brothers. Some became leaders in the church. Christians also at times emancipated slaves who were Christian brothers. Prisoners felt the mercy of caring believers. Brothers traveling to distant lands experienced Christian hospitality. In short, exhibiting the reality of Christ through changed and concerned lives was characteristic of early believers.

The early church was flexible in structure and organization. The gifts of the Spirit were stressed, but the manner in which they were utilized and organized varied. However, false teachers forced the church to adopt more definite patterns of organization. By the second century, the title "bishop" was frequently given to the principal leader in any urban area. He led in worship, preached, organized believers, and supervised the church in his city. He might have a number of associates who worked with him. The body of believers, perhaps meeting in several homes or other places throughout the city, had a voice in selecting its leaders.

Gradually other offices were established. Presbyters were local area pastors and preachers. Deacons continued to minister to the needy. A distinct, separate class of Christian leadership, the clergy, emerged, some of whom were supported financially by those whom they served.

The bishop in Rome became the most important leader of the church in the west. He headed a large and spiritually strong congregation, located in the capital of the empire. The church in Rome had a rich heritage of apostolic and post-apostolic leadership which wisely led the church and advised the outlying groups. Rome remained true to the faith in the face of heretical pressure. Is it any wonder that the prestige of the bishop of Rome rose in prominence?

Church councils, from the time of Acts 15 on, represent an important aspect of church life. Depending upon the local situation and needs of the day, councils varied from a few local representatives to large synodical gatherings representing large areas. The 250s witnessed the first major church councils.

Creeds took their place, too, as a feature of church life. In order to screen out false teachers and teaching, the church asked baptismal candidates questions as to their beliefs. The answers eventually became positive statements of doctrine, widely held by Christians. The best known theological statement, used in Rome, became the basis for the Apostles' Creed.

In every age, the New Testament has been vital to the Christian life. While the Old Testament was recognized by the church as authoritative from the first, the various New Testament books increasingly came to be regarded as equally inspired. They were used in public and private worship along with Old Testament books. The New Testament itself contains numerous indications that the writers regarded their own writings, and also the writings of others, as God-breathed. Early Christian writers, such as Justin and Irenaeus, quote from New Testament books as possessing an authoritative message from God. During this period the intrinsic quality of the New Testament books impressed itself upon Christians. It is not that the church decided what writings were to make up the New Testament. The books, in and of themselves, possessed the authority of the Holy Spirit. The church merely recognized this. This process of recognition, the selection of the canon of Scripture, was completed later in the fourth century.

God was building His church during these foundational years. As Christians of the twentieth century, we can be grateful for the faith, boldness, and obedience to the Great Commission with which these believers took the Gospel to the Roman world.

2

Building through Storm and Test

Time line   0   100   200   300   400   500   600

It was not easy to live for Jesus Christ in the early centuries. It has never been easy to serve Him. Building the church was accomplished in spite of problems, hardships, and bloodshed.

Heresies and Schisms

False ideas proved to be a serious difficulty in the building of the church. New Testament writings—Jude, Second Peter, and Revelation 2 and 3—warned of the dangers of false teachings. The church came to face war on two fronts: persecution from without, and heresy within. If internal strength is what it should be, external opposition will never overpower the church. Persecution hurt the early church in some ways; heresy hindered it greatly.

Gnosticism probably existed, in incipient form, from the early days of the church's existence. It reached a peak in the mid-second century. Gnosticism was built upon a combination of ideas taken from Judaism, Greek philosophy, Christianity, and mystical speculation. It varied from one place and leader to another; thus, it had no single creed or theological system. Fundamental to gnosticism was a belief that matter was evil and only the spirit was good. In order for matter-centered man to be related to a "pure-spirit" god, he must approach through intermediaries or emanations. In some Gnostic systems, one of the lower emanations was the creator God of the Old Testament. Jesus was a spiritual being who came to lift man from his matter-centered existence. To many Gnostics, Jesus was a phantom, not possessing a human body, which would have been evil, but only appearing to do so. Salvation was by mystic experience, the so-called *gnosis*. It was exclusive, in that only a select few could achieve this experience.

Marcion, a wealthy former member of the church in Rome in the mid-second century, began a sect related in belief to the Gnostics. He developed his own list of Scriptural books which rejected the Old Testament and attempted to purge the New Testament of all its Jewish elements. The Marcionite canon included Luke and ten of Paul's letters.

In the third century, another Gnostic-like group arose to challenge the church. Mani was a Persian who combined Jewish, Zoroastrian, Buddhist, and Christian ideas with his own, creating "Manichaeism." Mani believed himself to be the promised Paraclete. He wrote, nevertheless with skill and clarity and organized his followers effectively. Manichaeans believed in the essential evil of matter and in an ascetic strictness in dealing with it. Many intellectuals, including Augustine (before his conversion), were later drawn into this expansive movement.

Neo-Platonism was a religious-philosophical system with a stress on contemplation, union with the eternal, and ascetic practice. It too was a challenge to the early church.

The heretical Judaizing trend, so much a problem in Acts, Galatians, and elsewhere in the New Testament, continued to plague the church. Ebionism was the name given to this approach during its existence from the second century through the fifth. Ebionites believed that Jesus was a good man and an apt teacher but generally denied His deity. They stressed keeping the law and circumcision as the means to salvation.

Monarchianism also tried to explain the problem of the trinity and developed into a full-blown doctrinal heresy. Some Monarchians taught that the qualities of godliness came upon the man Jesus at His baptism, thus promoting Him to Messiahship. Others denied the full personality of the three persons of the trinity, instead teaching that they were only manifestations or expressions of the Godhead. This approach came to be called Sabellianism, after a leading proponent.

In Asia Minor another schism developed: Montanism. Montanus taught that he was the recipient of new revelation from the Paraclete. His "vision" emphasized a Second Coming of Christ to Asia Minor, spiritual gifts, and strict asceticism. Montanism was a reaction to the worldliness of the day, but its proposed answers were not always in harmony with the Bible or Christian truth.

Another ascetic group from the third century followed some Montanist approaches. The Novatianists, followers of Bishop Novatian, separated from the main body of Christians over the issue of what to do with those who had fallen away under persecution and wanted to return. Novatian believed that the church was in error allowing such persons to return to fellowship.

In the early fourth century the Donatists, followers of Donatus, a North African bishop, held to a rigorist position like that of the Novatianists. They were critical of those who surrendered up the Scriptures during persecution, rather than suffering as Christians. They developed into a distinct organization, continuing for 400 years.

The effects of these heretical movements were sometimes positive and sometimes negative. Positively, the church was forced to define the truth clearly. Matter is not inherently evil in the Christian faith. God's good creation may be misused by sinful man, but matter is not evil in itself. Conflict with heresy brought the Christian canon of Scripture into sharper focus. Doctrinal positions and organizational patterns were demanded by persons trying to discern truth from error.

On the other hand, thousands were led astray by the errors of the groups we have mentioned. Even at times within the church itself, false teaching and practices were spawned. The over-ascetic emphasis of the later church began in this era, as did trends toward the division of Christians into clergy and laity in ways not taught by the New Testament.

Early Writings and Leaders

To counter the error of the false teachers, men of God early built the Christian church with the pen. Greek was the first language used, but eventually the Latin of the western Mediterranean area also came into prominence.

Some of these early Christian leaders have been called "church fathers" by the Roman Catholic church because of their antiquity, learnedness, holiness, and orthodoxy. At times their opinions have been regarded more highly than Scripture itself, perhaps explaining why evangelicals have in some situations avoided or neglected these men. Unquestionably the early church fathers disappoint us at times in that they do not always speak as clearly or as biblically as we would like. They were products of their own times speaking to issues which they faced, not those which concern us. Still, they contributed both to the building of the church in their own day and to our understanding today.

The quality of writing declined in the late-first and early-second century. The writers were good men, rather than great men of writing skill. They were zealous, absorbed in the conflicts of their day and concerned with edifying the Christians.

Clement of Rome, writing about 97, was perhaps the earliest Christian writer apart from the New Testament. His letter to the Christians of Corinth urged harmony and obedience among the church members there. Ignatius of Antioch also wrote a number of letters, speaking about martyrdom, the primacy of Christ, and the unity of the church.

Two anonymous writings from this early period were the *Shepherd of Hermas* and the *Didache* or *Teaching*. *Hermas* was a widely circulated devotional work, stressing the purity of the Christian life and greatly loved by early Christians. *Didache* was a manual of church life and procedure. Apparently local groups took direction from this writing as to worship forms and methods. Thus, it is a valuable source today to show how the early church operated.

Polycarp of Smyrna, from the early second century, was an influential Christian leader and writer. His letter to the Philippians is a humble, direct work of Christian instruction. Polycarp had been a student of the Apostle John so he provided the church with a direct authoritative link with its past. At the games in Smyrna, the pagan crowds called for Polycarp's death. He was hunted down and pressured to deny Christ. His answer was, "Eighty-six years I have served Him and He never did me any wrong. How can I blaspheme my King who saved me?" He was burned at the stake for his faith.

When persecution hit the church, some of the able minds, believing that the pen is mightier than the sword, wrote defenses of the Christian position. These men, called apologists, wrote to reach non-Christians in places of authority, arguing that believers were innocent of alleged crimes and that Christianity was a reasonable faith.

Justin, mid-second century, was a philosopher converted to Christ by reading the Old Testament. His *Apology*, which defends Christianity from governmental and pagan attacks, was addressed to Emperor Antonius Pius. His *Dialogue with Trypho* presented the Gospel against Jewish objections. Justin was executed for the cause of Christ; therefore history has termed him Justin Martyr.

Others used the apologetic method to speak out to the world. Quadratus, Tatian, Athenagoras, and Theophilius stand in this noble tradition. They used the miracles, fulfilled prophecy, and the resurrection as proof of the validity of Christianity. They also described simply and accurately just who the Christians were and what they believed and did. They challenged inaccurate pagan prejudices against the church.

By the year 200, this problem of the heresies demanded the attention of Christian leaders and writers. These men, called polemicists, lived in the western part of the Empire. Their attacks against Gnosticism, Monarchianism, and other heresies helped to maintain the inner purity of the church. The writers of this period maintain that their positions are catholic, that is "universal," rather than narrowly sectarian and heretical.

Irenaeus grew up in Asia Minor, where he was a student of Polycarp. He moved to Gaul (modern France), where he became a leader of the church. His *Against Heresy* is a vigorous attack against Gnosticism and a positive statement of orthodox, Christian belief. His writings make frequent use of the New Testament, quoting it copiously.

Tertullian, a lawyer in North Africa, was converted to Christianity and used his clear, legal mind to express in Latin his opposition to falsehood. His work *On Idolatry* illustrates a fiery, even severe approach in opposing paganism. He had a deep sense of sin and commitment to Christ. He also criticized the church for laxity, and eventually became a Montanist in his opposition to the unhappy trend.

Cyprian, who lived in North Africa in the early third century, was the bishop of Carthage. Facing both persecution and heresy, Cyprian stressed church unity and order. In his work, *On the Unity of the Church,* he places emphasis upon the distinctive differences between clergy and laity, and upon the importance of the bishops. Thus he is sometimes termed the "Father of Sacerdotalism" or the "Father of a Special Priestly Class."

The city of Alexandria, Egypt, with its long-standing tradition in Greek education, became a center of Christian learning in the third century. The school begun there to educate the children of believers and converts from paganism produced some outstanding catechetical writers.

Clement of Alexandria headed the school in about 200. In his writings he sought to win readers from paganism, instruct Christians, and interpret the Scriptures. He attempted to present the Christian message in the Greek philosophical patterns popular in that day.

Origen, a student of Clement, succeeded him in the school. He was one of the greatest minds in the early Christian church. His works include *De Principia,* a systematic theological study; *Hexapla,* with its six columns of Greek and Hebrew versions of the Old Testament; and commentaries on much of the Bible. Origen developed "allegorizing" (finding hidden meanings in Scripture). He also held some theological views of dubious accuracy, so his contribution to the church was not entirely positive. This opened the door for abundant possibilities in reading "into" the Scriptures what one wished to find.

Persecution

As God built His church, persecution increasingly appeared. Relationship with the state is usually an important factor in church life. In the early years of Christianity, the church and Judaism were considered one in the eyes of the ruling Romans. The Jews were a licensed cult; therefore the Christians enjoyed at least some legal recognition.

But this early recognition disappeared and persecution erupted. Jesus had predicted this, when He said, "In the world you will have tribulation " (John 16:33). Christians were accused of anarchy when they left the state religion and refused to worship the emperor. In the eyes of the state, Christianity became a dangerous, illegal cult. Its adherents refused to live like others who engaged in immoral practices. Roman society was based on a debased worship of pleasure. Christians had higher aspirations. The pagan writer Caecilius denounced Christians for not attending sacred contests, for not eating meats and drink offered to idols, and for not attending public entertainments. His conclusion that they neither rose again after death nor really lived in the present was both inaccurate and inadequate. He didn't know what real life was!

Romans also persecuted Christians charging atheism because they couldn't conceive of a religion without temples and idols. They accused the church of cannibalism in a distorted view of the Lord's Supper, and charged immorality because of the Christians' secret meetings. Believers taught that men were equal before God, a dangerous doctrine which struck at the heart of the Roman social class system. Christians were enthusiasts who sang and rejoiced in God. Pagans could not understand their joy. The Christians often became scapegoats for troubles which surfaced within the empire.

The first manifestation of imperial persecution came in the reign of Nero in the 60s. The first half of Nero's reign was largely peaceful, but after the fire in Rome, probably begun accidentally, Christians were blamed and vigorously persecuted. Roman writer Tacitus tells that Christians were used to counteract the rumor that Nero himself set the fire. So believers were tortured, torn to pieces by dogs, and burned to death in Nero's gardens. This spate of hatred was demonstrated in Rome itself. Fortunately it did not spread too widely. Perhaps Paul and Peter lost their lives in this persecution.

A period of calm followed the persecution, thus allowing the church to regroup and rebuild. However, Emperor Domitian in the 80s and 90s again led a persecution of believers. In Rome, harried Christians met for worship in underground catacombs. In Asia Minor many believers lost their lives. Families were encouraged to spy on one another.

After the assassination of Domitian, relative peace prevailed for a time. Though it was illegal to serve Christ, local authorities often overlooked the law. The Church grew dramatically. Some Roman officials even shielded Christians from persecution. In the reign of Marcus Aurelius, 161-180, vigorous persecution again erupted, but a succeeding emperor was more tolerant so the church again thrived. One emperor even reputedly had a bust of

Christ in his private chapel so that he could consider Him along with all his other gods!

During the first years of its existence, the church was in real peril. Comparatively few Christians, however, actually died for their faith. Persecutions were local and intermittent. Too often it is assumed that persecution was a great benefit to the church in keeping it pure, instilling courage and building faith. A measure of truth exists in these ideas. However, had Rome, with its might, determined early to wipe out the Gospel, from a human perspective, she would have succeeded. But God, in His providence, did not allow this to take place. Rome's persecutions were spasmodic and never great enough to stop the building of His church.

In the mid-third century, however, the tempo of opposition picked up tragically. Paganism revived with the celebration of the 1000th anniversary of the founding of Rome. Christians were blamed for urging people to forsake the old gods, thus causing the problems of the day. In the reign of Decius, 249-251, the first general persecution of the church was carried out. Christians all over the empire were forced to possess certificates stating that they had sacrificed to the pagan gods. If they did not, they were tortured or put to death. The successors of Decius continued this policy. Churches were scattered, leaders executed. Providentially, after 260 a more tolerant policy prevailed so that the church could survive.

In 284, Diocletian came to the Roman throne. A slave by birth, this unusual man rose through the ranks of the army to the emperorship. But the empire was tottering; its economic and social foundations were in peril. Outside forces were pressuring its borders. Feeling that Christians would make a useful scapegoat for Rome's problems, Diocletian issued a series of edicts instituting the second general persecution of the church. Copies of the Scriptures, by now widely distributed, were confiscated and destroyed. The older, military camp-type paganism was encouraged. Many believers lost their lives.

A period of conflict and civil strife followed, involving power struggles among rival claimants to the throne. From the first, Christians favored a young general in the west, Constantine. In 312 Constantine confronted only one rival in his quest for control of the west. Constantine claimed a vision in the afternoon before the Battle of Mulvian Bridge. In obedience to the vision, he had his troops place the sign of the cross on their standards as they marched into battle. The battle won, the empire was his. The following year Constantine issued the Edict of Milan which gave official toleration to the church. At last the Christians had peace and freedom. The building of the church now could proceed without governmental persecution. As subsequent events were to demonstrate, however, this blending of church and state was not always a beneficial one to building God's church.

3

Building Under Government Pressure

Time line   200   300   400   500   600   700   800   900

With the end of persecution by the government, the church now faced great opportunity for development. At some points, Rome actually helped in building. On other occasions its role could be more accurately described as interference.

The Government's Position

Constantine saw Christianity as a means of unifying a steadily fragmenting empire. He encouraged the erection of church buildings at significant sites. He passed laws helpful to Christians. He began a policy of settling church disputes by calling leaders together under imperial direction. It is difficult to know just how deep, sincere, and genuine Constantine's personal Christianity was.

Constantine's successors generally followed his pro-Christian policies. Julian the Apostate, 361-363, was an exception in that he tried to revive heathenism. It was a lost cause. Christianity grew to dominance. So strong was the influence of the church, that Emperor Theodosius in 380

31

issued an edict which made Christianity the only legal religion of the Roman Empire. Any one who would dare to hold another faith would now be liable to Roman persecution. How dramatically events had changed in less than 100 years! Laws were passed against pagans. So-called Christians persecuted non-Christians!

The Roman Empire came into a period of decline in the late fourth century. Internal corruption and decay gradually sapped the vitality of the state. The end was hastened by Germanic peoples, called "barbarians," harassing the empire from the north.

The Goths made frequent raids into imperial territory in the east. They thoroughly defeated a Roman army at Adrianople in 378 and later moved into portions of Greece, Italy, and Spain, founding temporary or semi-permanent "kingdoms." A resident of Asia Minor, Ulfilas, however, continued to assist in building the church even in these difficult days. Captured by Gothic raiders, he had opportunity to learn the ways of these nomadic peoples. After his release, he determined to go back to tell them of Christ. Like captive American prisoners of war in World War II, who returned to Japan to tell their captors of the Savior, Ulfilas became the "Apostle to the Goths." He taught and preached. He wrote and translated the Scriptures into Gothic. Later, when members of this tribal group invaded the empire, some of them were already Christians.

The Vandals, who eventually occupied the Carthage area of North Africa, greatly weakened Roman rule in many areas of the west. They may have been responsible for eliminating the puppet, nominal ruler, Romulus Augustulus, in Rome in 476.

The Franks and Burgundians moved into modern France in the late 400s and early 500s. A Christian confronted

Clovis, their chief, with the story of Christ. Moved by the story, Clovis became a Christian. Since he believed that what is good for a chief is good for his people, he marched some 3,000 of his men through a river, supposedly "baptizing" them as Christians!

In successive waves, the Angles, Saxons, and Jutes swept over the British Isles. The church there was driven northward and westward, unable to contend effectively with the pagan onslaught. The Huns also created serious difficulty for some established Christian communities on the continent.

The collapse of Roman civilization and the infusion of Germanic culture slowed the building of the church. Gradually, these invaders were assimilated into Greco-Roman communities and became nominally Christian. The church assisted in the preservation of civilized forms, converted these pagans to Christianity, and helped educate them. From this fusion of Greco-Roman and Germanic elements grew western civilization. However, the purity of the witness of the church was seriously corrupted by the barbarian absorption. Many of the converts wore only the thinnest of Christian veneer and knew nothing of a vital, new-birth experience.

Theology

The period of the imperial state church of the 400s and 500s was extremely important in the establishment of doctrine. The theological formulas which were developed helped to preserve the church's doctrine.

The first controversy over the deity of Christ shook the Christian community in that period. Arius, a presbyter from Antioch, taught that Christ was the first being to come from the creative hand of God. He was godly in a sense, but not God in essence or from eternity. In the incarnation, this previously-created being entered human flesh as Jesus of Nazareth. Arius gathered followers, especially across the east. His opponents, those who insisted upon the full deity of Jesus Christ, taught that Arianism was a dangerous heresy affecting the very heart of Christianity.

At Nicea, in Asia Minor, in 325, a General Council was held to discuss the matter. Emperor Constantine, hating the disunity which the controversy produced, urged a solution to the problem. Eventually Alexander, Athanasius, and others favoring the orthodox position were able to secure the adoption of a credal statement proclaiming Jesus Christ as of the same essence as the Father. This statement came to be the heart of what we call the Nicean Creed today.

Arianism was not dead, however. It took time before all segments of the church supported the Nicean position. Church Basil, Gregory of Nyssa, and Gregory of Nazianzus preached, wrote, and taught the truth. In addition, Emperor Theodosius gave full government support. Thus the biblical position on the full deity of Christ prevailed.

A second controversy developed concerning the relationship between the divine and the human elements in Jesus Christ. How could Jesus be both fully God and fully man?

In Alexandria, Egypt, men like Apollinaris, Cyril of Alexandria, and others overemphasized the unity of the two natures, human and divine, in Jesus with the result that the understanding of His true humanity was blurred. In Antioch, Syria, Theodore of Mopsuestia, Nestorius, and others emphasized the division of the two natures to such a degree that the unity of His person was neglected. Arguments raged. Personality clashes surfaced. Political advantage at times was more important than biblical truth. An aged monk, called Eutyches, added a further dimension to the Alexandrian position by stating that a third nature, not the same as either human or divine, was produced in the incarnation. Eventually Nestorius was condemned and banished. His followers, incidentally, became a missionary force reaching to the east as far as China.

Another General Council was held at Chalcedon, in Asia Minor, in 451. At that council, the views of the western part of the church, as expressed in the *Tome* written by Leo I, the bishop of Rome, were adopted. The Chalcedonian Creed which resulted was a balanced position which defined the full humanity and full deity of Christ as coming together in one person. It was a helpful statement which avoided the extremes of either Alexandria or Antioch and which has served the church well ever since.

Still, the arguments were not over. Followers of the Alexandrian position, called Monophysites, formed their own churches. The Coptic churches in Egypt and Ethiopia today are descendants of this group. Another group tried to assert that while Jesus had two natures, He had only one will and that divine. However the main body of believers came to accept the Chalcedon formula. It has been the position of Protestant, Eastern Orthodox, and Roman Catholic churches in modern times.

A third controversy centered around the question of the nature of man. Pelagius was an austere monk who taught that man is essentially free and is able to do that which he ought to do. He denied the then-current concept of original sin. Pelagius believed that Adam's fall was but a bad example which men have followed. To him, man's own efforts were vital to the salvation process.

In opposition, Augustine wrote strongly that regeneration was a work exclusively of God. Man's will was entirely corrupted by the fall and could not produce salvation. This can come to man only through the grace of

Christ to those who are the elect.

At the General Council of 431 held in Ephesus (one of six such gatherings which wielded wide influence in the church of this period), Pelagianism was condemned. The teaching that man can achieve salvation by his own efforts, however, has repeatedly reappeared to challenge the church.

While these theological controversies slowed the church-building process by turning men's attention to winning arguments, these well-worded doctrinal statements did much to draw careful theological boundaries around truth. These great creeds have been in use ever since.

Church Life

The average churchman then, as now, was more likely to be concerned about his own local situation than about remote theological argument. Church services were held frequently and were important to Christian growth. Singing by congregation and choir was a joyful part of worship. Great preaching flourished. Audiences responded to sermon points with vigorous applause. The sacraments were increasingly important. Special times of the year, such as Christmas and Easter, were observed with considerable emphasis.

After persecution stopped a new danger confronted the church. The converted pagans tended to view the martyrs as special heroes and believed they had special powers of intercession. The result was the tragic increase in the practice of saint worship. Mary, the mother of Jesus, was regarded as the highest of the saints. She became the sympathetic mediator as Jesus was erroneously viewed primarily as a harsh judge. Relics of biblical times or of the saints were revered. In the east sacred pictures, or icons, became the objects of veneration. These practices greatly endangered the purity of the church.

Organizationally, bishops and other members of the hierarchy grew in influence and power. The bishop of Rome continued to exert a widespread influence and prominence in the west. Early in the fifth century Innocent I claimed supremacy for the Roman bishopric over other bishops, although not all agreed with him. Celibacy became the ideal for clergymen, especially in the west. This was not universally practiced at this time, however, as the eastern church maintained a strong married-clergy tradition.

Monastic asceticism developed prominently in the imperial state church era. At first devout men merely lived highly ascetic lives within the church community. Then the practice developed of withdrawing from the world as hermits into solitary places for meditation and prayer. As more like-minded people moved nearby, a cloister was built where they could live and work in common. Finally a full communal monastery system was established.

Monasticism did not originate with Christianity. Buddhistic and Jewish practice had developed it before the time of Christ. But with the declining ethical and religious standards of the church at large, serious people wanted something better than they had. So separation from the world through contemplative, monastic life seemed the answer.

The Egyptian, Anthony, (250-356?) has been called the Father of Christian Monasticism." At age eighteen, he gave up property and friends and became a hermit in the desert. He was widely imitated. Pachomius, about 315-320, established the first Christian monastery, located in southern Egypt.

At times abuses developed. Simon Stylites spent thirty years on top of a pillar in Syria to show his devotion.

Monks engaged in other fanatic practices as well. Some eastern monks were unruly and unwilling to accept any church discipline.

Generally, however, monasticism was organized and disciplined by good men. Benedict of Nursia was outstanding in this respect. At Monte Cassino monastery in Italy he developed his *Rule,* which spelled out how life should be lived. The *Rule* divided life into specific periods for labor, study, and prayer. Some of the best men of the centuries to follow were the monks. They were often the preservers of biblical truths and ideals which the church as a whole had neglected.

Leaders and Writers

The imperial state church era was the golden age of the church fathers. Some great leaders appeared at this time—men of courage, genius, and faith.

Athanasius, 295-373, the defender of orthodoxy against Arianism, was a man of great character and strong conviction. He would not compromise his beliefs even though it cost him exile and banishment five different times. The valor of Athanasius was a prime reason why Nicean theology ultimately won the day.

Ambrose, 340-397, was drafted, in spite of great personal reluctance, to the position of bishop of Milan. He emphasized worship in his ministry by his own skillful preaching and by the development of church music. Administratively, Ambrose worked to unity the previously divided Christians of his area. He boldly insisted upon righteous behavior, even from Emperor Theodosius, whom he excommunicated from the church for his massacre of 7,000 Thessalonians.

Augustine, 354-430, represents a high point of the

ancient church. Although his mother was a Christian, young Augustine lived a rebellious licentious life. A keen student, he devoted his energies to the study of the philosophies of the day. After a dramatic conversion, Augustine became a clergyman and eventually a bishop in North Africa. His writings were prolific and influential. His *Confessions,* telling his life story, reveals deep personal piety. His *City of God,* a philosophy of history, shaped much medieval thinking. His theology is a blend of contrasting emphases. He placed stress upon the imperative necessity of God's elective grace in bringing man to salvation and also upon the church and the sacraments as the vehicles whereby that grace is dispensed. Both Protestants and Roman Catholics have drawn upon Augustine in developing their theologial positions.

One of the greatest Bible scholars of the ancient church was Jerome, 346-420, an ardent advocate of the monastic life. Jerome built a monastery in Bethlehem where he engaged in his greatest work, the translation of the Bible into Latin. The result was the so-called Vulgate or common version. His Vulgate became THE Bible of the church in the west for 1,000 years. Argumentative Jerome also wrote commentaries on the Scripture and theological works.

Chrysostom, 347-407, was one of the great orator-preachers of the ancient church. As bishop of Constantinople, he opposed sin at all levels. He did not spare even the empress in his denunciations. His communication skills were vigorous and effective. Actually, his name was John, but history has termed him Chrysostom, or "Golden Mouth," because of his powerful preaching.

Leo I, the Great, was bishop of Rome from 440 to 461. His theological statement, the *Tome,* assisted in the solution of the controversy over the two natures in Christ. He also assisted in the governing of central Italy when secular authority had broken down under barbarian pressure. Leo strongly asserted claims for papal supremacy, basing his arguments upon the concept of Petrine supremacy and Matthew 16:18. His influence was great.

Gregory the Great was bishop of Rome from 590 to 604. Problems plagued the city during his leadership—floods, barbarian invasions, disease, hunger. Gregory proved a capable administrator, assisting the people of the city in these crises. Increasingly political concerns were forced upon him. In church life, Gregory emphasized preaching, often using the judgmental-type style then popular. He assisted in modifying the musical forms then in use, thus creating the Gregorian chant. The emphasis on tradition as authoritative along with the Bible, the practice of penance, and belief in purgatory indicate that the church was moving, theologically into a different path from what it had first followed. Gregory's theology is often thought of as the beginning of the medieval church.

It is apparent that this period of the church's history saw both the gold, silver, and precious stones (sound theology, missionary outreach, and earnest living) and the wood, hay, and stubble (saint worship, works, unbiblical theology). The era must be assessed in a balanced way. The church survived every threat either from the state or any other human instrumentalities.

4

Building When the Culture Collapses

Time line   400   500   600   700   800   900   1000   1300

Very few religions outlast their cultures. When a culture collapses, its religion generally falls too. Such was not the case with the disintegration of the Roman system. The Christian church not only survived, but preserved many of the values of Greco-Roman society.

The titles "medieval" or "Middle Ages" are names given to the next period we shall consider. Historians have dated the beginning of the period from 300 to 600 and the conclusion from 1200 to 1600. For our purposes, the one thousand years from 500 to 1500 provide a convenient way to remember the era. We shall study this period in chapters four and five.

Was God building His church in this time? If so, how? The answers to these questions are much more difficult to ascertain for the medieval era than for any other period. Sometimes writers have referred to these years as the "Dark Ages" because of the corruption, secularization, and false doctrine which developed in the church.

Yet, God was not left without a witness, even in these years. At times, we must take that concept as a matter of

41

faith rather than history. The evidence of light is slim; darkness abounds. But the essence of the history of the church, the body of Christ, lies with individual lives, not in the great institutions bearing the name "Christian."

The ancient church father, Clement of Alexandria, compared the church to a great river, sometimes flowing vigorously and openly, like a great flood, and at other times silently going underground. In the Middle Ages, while the framework of the church stood solidly, the real body of Christ may well have gone "underground" in the lives of individuals. Believers were scattered in monasteries and in local churches. Some were in the organized church and others were in dissenting groups. Though construction may have seemed slow and scattered, God was still building His church.

Expansion

The British Isles were the site of an exciting expansion of the church in the early Middle Ages. While the Gospel had penetrated that area in Roman times, the Anglo-Saxon invasions of the 500s virtually wiped out the church.

Patrick, who was to become known as the "Apostle to the Irish," was a young Scotsman who was taken to Ireland by force and made a slave. After being converted to Christ while tending swine, he escaped. He studied at a monastery in southern France and then experienced a Macedonian-like call. An Irishman was pleading with him, "Please, holy boy, come and walk among us again."

Moved by the experience, Patrick returned to Ireland. He became the evangelist, preacher, and teacher for the island, greatly loved by the people. Although much mythical material has grown up around his life, it is likely that his *Confessions* is a true representation of his life and beliefs.

Building When the Culture Collapses 43

In many respects his work was closer to the earlier Christian patterns than to the medieval Romanistic forms which were to develop.

Columba was called the "Apostle to Scotland." With his base at the monastery at Iona, he, together with his associates, won the Scots and Picts for Christ. Areas of northern England and even sections of the continent were reached by men of British or Celtic tradition. Without influence from the outside, Christians of the British Isles re-evangelized large segments of their lands.

Pope Gregory the Great, around 600, sent Augustine as a missionary to the British Isles. (This is not the same Augustine as the great church father who lived 150 years earlier.) The local Christians clashed with this Roman intruder, but eventually harmony prevailed and the British church submitted to Roman leadership.

On the continent, Boniface, the "Apostle to the Germans," evangelized, organized, and civilized that land. When he chopped down the sacred oak tree at Geismar, the pagans expected him to be struck dead. His bravery provided an opening for the Gospel. He was murdered while baptizing some of his converts.

Anskar, in the early 800s, attempted to win the Scandinavian people to Christianity. Mystical and ascetic, he opened the northland to the church. But it wasn't until the kings of that region responded that the majority of the peoples became Christians. Denmark was largely Christianized in the 900s, Norway in the 1000s, Sweden in the 1100s, and Finland even later.

To the east, Cyril and Methodius, two brothers, traveled in the 800s to what is now western Czechoslovakia. They invented a Slavic script, translated Bible portions, and won many to Christianity. As in the north, kings were largely responsible for bringing eastern lands to the church. King

Boris of Bulgaria in the 800s, Stephen I of Hungary in the 1000s, and Boleslaus I of Poland in the 1000s played significant roles in this process.

Queen Olga and her grandson, Vladimir I of Russia, were baptized in the 900s. Their subjects followed. Although Vladimir's personal life was anything but upright, he has been termed a saint because he led the nation to Christianity. Emissaries visited both Rome and Constantinople and chose to follow eastern patterns of worship because they were believed more beautiful. Thus Russia was, from the beginning, allied with what was to become Eastern Orthodox Christianity. The depth of religious life in this period was superficial and shallow.

Rural areas in the former Roman Empire lands were often slow to accept Christianity. Consistent teaching eventually won these lands. The English term "pagan" stems from a word meaning "dweller in rural areas."

Thus, Europe was largely Christianized by the year 1000. In some instances this missionary work had biblical foundations and resulted in solid, Christian lives. In most cases, it would appear, the conversions were to a system or to an organization. Only a nominal and sacramental Christianity developed, overlying the paganism which still remained.

While the church was growing in the north Islam was invading the south bringing great losses to Christianity. Mohammed was born in 570. By his death in 632, he had won the loyalty of the Arab peoples of the Arabian peninsula. Imbued with religious zeal and military skill, they overran the formerly Christian lands of the southeast. Palestine and Syria, Egypt and the Carthage area were in Arab hands by 700. In 711 the Arabs crossed Gibralter and soon conquered Spain. Crossing the Pyrenees, they even ravaged France for a time, until Charles Martel defeated them in the Battle of Tours in 732.

As the Arabs occupied more and more territory, the churches in these lands fell steadily into decline. Some Christians fled, others denied the faith, some were killed. Christian communities became distinct, ingrown ghettos, with little or no evangelistic outreach. The previous lack of biblical teaching and the resultant weakness in spiritual power had left the churches unable to cope with the onslaught of Islam. The great Christian centers of Alexandria, Jerusalem, and Antioch became islands in a vast Islamic sea. The church has never regained a strong position in the lands of North Africa or the Near East.

Papacy and Government

In the early Middle Ages, the Roman popes used alliances with the Frankish kings to their advantage. Pippin the Short was crowned by Pope Stephen II in 754. He returned the favor by giving the papacy Italian territory which he had taken from another ruler. Thus began the Papal States, a political realm ruled by popes and demanding their time, interest, and money. The Donation of Constantine, later proven to be a forgery, was used to support this territorial arrangement. By this document, Constantine supposedly had granted wide territorial rule to the papacy.

Pippin's son, Charlemagne, conquered a vast territory in western Europe. In addition to being an able military man and civil administrator, Charlemagne took a vital interest in the church. Charlemagne established schools for the clergy to combat the overwhelming illiteracy of the period. He organized the church, appointed bishops, and encouraged monasteries. His life illustrates the contradictions of the era—deep interest in religion and careful observance of its forms combined with military cruelty and immorality.

At Charlemagne's death, his vast empire collapsed. Wandering local bands and raiders like the Normans, Saracens, and Hungarians fostered unstable conditions. Society turned inward and emphasized feudal, local political and social arrangements. The church reemphasized the local parish in this period and became the focal point of many a village across Europe.

The late 800s and early 900s were dark years for church administration. The papacy fell under the control of unscrupulous Romans whose debauched lives disgraced the church. Between 896 and 904 ten popes occupied the papal throne. Pope John XII, just prior to his elevation to office, made a drunken toast to the devil. Steven VI was strangled. The remains of Formosus were disinterred, dressed in robes in a court, and condemned. John VIII was poisoned, beaten with a hammer, and dragged through Rome. Three women dominated the papacy for a time. Benedict IX sold the papal office to the highest bidder.

Finally the emerging power of the German Emperors, the so-called Holy Roman Emperors, intervened to restore stability and decency in the headquarters of the church. It is tragic that the church could not maintain the order of its own house and that secular authority had to step in to do so. Further problems developed because the German emperors frequently exercised control over church affairs, particularly the appointment of men to high church positions. One type of evil had been corrected, in that men of upright personal life led the church. Another evil replaced it, secular control of the church.

Leo IX served as pope from 1049 to 1054. He was an earnest churchman, zealous for reforming the papacy. During his tenure of office, he opposed secular appointment of church officers, clerical marriages, and the sale of church offices. He appointed reformers, like himself, to places of leadership. Leo was, therefore, a strong leader in an era when vigorous direction at the head of the church was often lacking.

In one matter, however, Leo IX's papacy produced failure rather than success. For years relations between the patriarch of Constantinople and the pope at Rome had been deteriorating. Personal jealousies, cultural and language differences, relations with secular government, and differences in church practice had divided them. In 1054, Leo excommunicated the Constantinople patriarch, Michael Cerularius, and his followers. The patriarch returned the favor in the same year. Although many years were to pass before this division was structured and formalized, east and west had gone their separate ways. Distinct Eastern Orthodox and Roman Catholic traditions resulted.

Secular involvement in church appointments continued to be a problem. Since the church had come to control much land and since archbishops were powerful secular lords in addition to being religious leaders, the kings reasoned they needed men loyal to them in order to govern their realms. But the papacy claimed that the archbishops were primarily churchmen and therefore must give their loyalty to the pope. This conflict was termed the investiture controversy, that is, should secular or religious leaders invest appointees to their offices. The issue affected even the selection of popes.

The controversy came to a climax in the papacy of Gregory VII, or Hildebrand, 1073-1085. Gregory was a brilliant and demanding pope who believed in the absolute supremacy of the papacy in all things. When the archbishopric of Milan became vacant, Gregory had a dispute with Henry IV over the appointment of a successor.

48 *Built upon the Cornerstone*

And though Henry was the ruler of Germany and northern Italy, Gregory excommunicated him from the church. This eventuality was just what Henry's political enemies were waiting for. Henry, trying desperately to maintain his position as king, stood for three days barefoot in the snow at Gregory's Canossa castle begging for absolution. Finally Gregory relented and released the king. Henry was able to maintain authority in his kingdom, but the event made the papacy seem more powerful than secular rulers. Canossa represented a high-water mark of papal power and authority.

Another example of medieval papacy power came in the rule of Innocent III, 1198-1216. He supported Frederick II in his quest for the throne of the Holy Roman Empire (Germany), insisted that the kings of France and Spain not divorce their wives, opposed heretics, and improved clerical education. In a contest with King John of England over investiture, Innocent placed that land under interdict, which forebade the observance of any religious rites. In 1215, Innocent called the Fourth Lateran Council into session. One of the most significant actions of that council was the declaration that the belief in transubstantiation must be held by all the faithful. Transubstantiation was the belief that the bread and wine of the communion become, to the eye of faith and when duly consecrated by a priest, the actual body and blood of Christ. It had been a view widely held in the church before; now it was to be mandatory. Innocent was the most powerful man of his age.

Church Life

In the early Middle Ages, the average churchman was ill educated, doctrinally ignorant, and unspiritual. Church life was at a low ebb. It was easy to transfer the worship of

Martin Luther

Quaker Meeting

John Wesley Preaching

The Catacombs

pagan deities to the saints or angels. Relics and pageantry were widely loved. Processions carrying the cross wended their way through the streets of European villages. Masses were said for the dead. Holy water was sprinkled on the sick. Relics supposedly worked miraculous cures. Little clerical learning or theological advance occurred.

Students of church history often ask when the Roman Catholic church came into being. No single date can be assigned to that development. The distinctive beliefs and practices which have served to identify the Roman church were gradually added to church practice. Different areas and leaders varied in their acceptance of these beliefs. While we are reluctant to term the church "Roman Catholic" in ancient church history, by the early medieval period the term fits thoroughly. By 800, and probably a century or two prior to that in many areas, Roman Catholicism could be said to exist.

The eastern segment of the church, which did not recognize the Roman pontiff, was characterized by a strong tie between the Byzantine emperors and the patriarchs of Constantinople. Magnificent, elaborate liturgical services were held, featuring many prayers, readings, musical chants, and sermons.

A major controversy developed in the east in the 700s over the use of religious pictures or icons. Emperor Leo III tried to ban the veneration of icons, but the monks and common people clung to them. A tumultuous period followed, involving army action, papal interference, and murder. The Seventh General Council, Nicea, in 787, the last of the ancient councils, approved the use of icons for reverential respect, but not for worship.

The Crusades were one of the most popular elements of medievel life. The Holy Land had fallen into the hands of the infidel Muslims. Christians were stirred to attempt a rescue. And on the side, they were pleased with the prospect of adventure, plunder, travel, and fame.

In 1095, the eastern emperor appealed to Pope Urban II for assistance. Urban was caught up in the idea of giving aid, so he urged the formation of a crusade. (The term is taken from the Latin word crux or cross, so a Crusader is one who bears the cross.) Feudal nobility raised armies and captured Jerusalem in 1099 in a terrible slaughter. The Latin Kingdom of Jerusalem was established, patterned after western European practices, whether they fit the east or not.

Western military and governmental strength in the east tended to erode through the decades, so new crusades were promoted to strengthen the Latin Kingdom. Some were disasters. The Fourth Crusade sacked Christian Constantinople and never did fight any Muslims. The Children's Crusade of 1212 saw 30,000 French children, led by a boy of twelve, set out on a crusading venture. Thousands died; others were sold into slavery. The Sixth Crusade was led by an emperor who had little or no religious interest.

Finally by 1291, western holdings in Palestine were completely lost. The direct objective of the Crusaders to bring the Holy Land under Christian control had failed. Some stimulation of intellectual and commercial life may have been accomplished by the Crusades, however. The church was affected in that the papacy was strengthened by the movement. In addition, a spirit of intolerance and hatred was bred. The ideal of killing your enemy was encouraged by the crusading movement. Perhaps as many as one million Christians and Muslims lost their lives. The Inquisition was born in this spirit.

Much of the material in this chapter may seem to have little to do with the building of God's church. Unbiblical practices and unspiritual behavior predominate. It may well be, however, that the underground river of the true church flowed in the monasteries, places of retreat and prayer.

Periodically, the monastic movement experienced renewals of vitality and purpose, as in the Cluniac reform in France in the 900s and the Cistercian movement in the 1100s. The Cistercians lived very strict lives in houses far out in the countryside. Lengthy private prayer schedules dominated their days. The most important Cistercian, Bernard of Clairvaux, 1090-1153, was an interesting combination of mystical and moral piety and administrative forcefulness. Bernard dominated the papacy and promoted crusading. He also wrote devotional sermons and poems. He was the author of the Latin hymn which stands behind our hymns "Jesus the Very Thought of Thee" and "Jesus, Thou Joy of Loving Hearts."

The Dominican order was founded in the early 1200s by the Spaniard Dominic. Committed to poverty, the Dominicans were mendicant, or begging friars. Their special emphasis was upon education and teaching, whereby they sought to overcome the prevailing ignorance of the time. They became the dominant order of the schools and universities.

Francis of Assisi, 1182-1226, founded the Franciscan order. After a riotous youth, Francis was converted to the religious life. He and his followers strongly stressed poverty, identifying with the poor masses of people in their travels and ministry. They emphasized living Christianity by example. Many myths grew up around the life of Francis, including the belief that he died having the stigmata, or wounds of Christ, in his body. We still use his poem "Eternal Life."

Doubtless many persons who truly committed their lives

to Christ lived and died in obscurity in this period. Although outward appearances may not tell us so, we believe that God was not defeated. He continued to build His church in spite of tremendous obstacles.

5

Building in Dark Days

Time line   900   1000   1100   1200   1300   1400   1600

In the high Middle Ages, or the latter half of the 1000 years arbitrarily termed "medieval," the trend of substituting man's opinion and tradition for biblical truth continued in the church. Early medieval practices expanded and developed. Still, God was at work, building His church in "underground river" kinds of places.

Elements of Vitality

Devout men in Germany, who have been termed the "mystics," may well have been a part of that building process. The mystics looked for direct spiritual experience. They saw the church as overwhelmingly external and ritualistic and wanted direct communion with God. As a result, they developed the "mystic way" to knowing God. First they sought purity from this world's sin. Then they attempted to understand His will and way through surrender of their lives to God. Then they experienced a mystical union with God wherein they walked in His light. Some of the mystics may be faulted for overly ascetic and human approaches to Christianity. However, others seem to have discovered much of the biblical pattern of knowing

53

God personally.

Meister Eckhart, 1260-1327, was the chief founder of German mysticism. A Dominican monk and busy administrator of 50 monasteries, Eckhart also was an effective preacher in the German vernacular who placed great stress upon the reality of God in the soul. In some areas, however, his theology was questionable.

His disciple, John Tauler, was a humble man who ministered well to the common German peasants. His message was strongly touched by biblical and evangelical content. Martin Luther, later, found his writings of great value in assisting him to faith.

The anonymous devotional writing, *German Theology*, expresses some of the strong elements of the mystic movement.

The Brethren of the Common Life was a lay monastic teaching organization which gave the movement some organizational foundation. The Brethren combined intellectual diligence with devotional warmth. They also taught the Bible in the vernacular and insisted upon a strong practical emphasis for daily life.

The most famous member of the Brethren of the Common Life was Thomas á Kempis, 1380-1471. This shy, peasant copyist of Scripture lived an uneventful life, but has influenced thousands through his writing, *The Imitation of Christ*. To Thomas, Jesus was the essence of the Christian life and had to have absolute supremacy in all concerning the believer. His work has been read by Protestant and Roman Catholic alike through the succeeding centuries.

The church demonstrated vitality, too, in its missionary outreach in the later Middle Ages. Ramon Lull, 1232?-1315, served faithfully for many years among the Muslims of what is now Tunisia, only to see little visible fruit for his labors and to be stoned to death when he was more than eighty. His upright example, however, provided a model which was greatly admired in that period. Franciscan and Dominican monks covered much of North Africa with missionary outreach.

The famous visit of the Polos to China stimulated European interest in the Far East. As a result, churchmen also renewed activity there. Franciscan monk, John of Monte Corvino, began a church in Peking in 1300. Others ministered in other parts of the orient.

Muslim influence continued to expand in the Near East, however. In the fourteenth century, the Turks pushed aggressively into western Asia Minor, already weakened by the plundering of the crusades. They crossed over into the Balkan peninsula in southeastern Europe. In 1453, their forces entered the city of Constantinople itself. On May 29, 1453, the Byzantine emperor, the patriarch of Constantinople, and other leaders realizing the end was near held a communion service in St. Sophia Cathedral. The next day, the victorious Turks held a Muslim thanks service in the same building. It was symbolic. Constantinople, which formerly had been an important center of eastern Christendom, was now a Muslim center. The eastern church now looked to Russia for its center of strength.

Not all Christians were members of churches which were within the Roman system. The ancient church had experienced divisions and separations. In spite of rigorous organization and pressure to the contrary, the Middle Ages also experienced independent renewal and schismatic groups.

Some of the separatists were biblical; but others were more heretical than the main body of Christendom. The Cathari or Albigenses, for example, spread widely across France, Italy, and Spain in the twelfth and thirteenth centuries, winning a majority of the populations in some areas. Their doctrine repeated the ancient gnostic ideas of the evil nature of matter. The Cathari were severely persecuted by the Roman church, which instituted a crusade against them. Cities were sacked, areas depopulated.

In contrast, groups appeared which attempted to restore a biblical basis to Christianity. Followers of Peter of Bruys, Henry of Lausanne, and Arnold of Brescia, all in the 1100s, stressed the authority of the Scriptures as opposed to church tradition. Perhaps the true body of Christ, the "underground church," may have been found, in part, among these groups.

The best known of these evangelical separatists were the Waldensians, followers of Peter Waldo. Peter was a merchant in Lyons, France. His heart was troubled by abuses he saw in the church, so he began to preach Bible truths. His followers came to be called the "Poor Men of Lyons," because of his strong emphasis on poverty. Gradually they applied the Bible to other areas of doctrine and life. The papacy opposed the Waldensians, but the group remained, later joining with the Protestants of the Reformation era. Remnants survive in Italy and elsewhere today.

Intellectual Life

The high Middle Ages were anything but "dark" in terms of intellectual expression. Learning rebounded significantly from the low ebb it faced in the early medieval period. The church played a signigicant role in this revival.

The monasteries were centers of learning in the Middle Ages. So also were the schools which developed in the large cathedrals. In the twelfth and thirteenth centuries, universities developed out of the monastic or cathedral schools. Other universities developed informally around great teachers or were established by governments. By 1400, more than seventy-five universities existed across Europe. Paris, Oxford, Cambridge, Salerno, and Bologna were among the most famous. Since printing was not yet developed, books were scarce and expensive. The schools were a part of the history of the church in that theology was the "Queen of the sciences" and accorded a central place in the curriculum. Church leaders and thinkers increasingly trained in the universities.

Scholasticism came to be the principal approach used in medieval intellectual inquiry. The scholastic method attempted to bring reason to support the Christian faith through the use of the philosophical forms of Aristotle and the other ancient Greeks. It was not that new doctrine was produced by the scholastic method; it was just that previously held beliefs were systematized and organized. Dominican monks played a vital role in the process.

Anselm of Canterbury, 1033-1109, has been called the "Father of the Scholastics." Although he was a strong administrator, Anselm is best remembered for his theology. In his book, *Why the God-Man?*, Anselm taught that Christ's death was a satisfaction of God's holiness which only He could pay. He spelled out intellectual proofs for the existence of God and yet insisted that faith must precede intellectual understanding of truth.

His chief opponent was Abelard, 1079-1142. Charming but arrogant, Abelard thrived on debate. His doctrine had elements which were heretical, so he became a hunted man. His personal life was equally stormy. Still his writings carried influence.

Peter Lombard was the author of the *Four Books of*

Sentences, which became the dominant theology text of the period.

The high point of scholasticism was the work of Thomas Aquinas, 1225-1274. An Italian by birth Thomas joined the Dominican order and became a teacher in the universities. His scholastic expressions of doctrine were done so thoroughly that his *Summa Theologia* became the definitive work on doctrine for years to follow. Thomas not only taught the orthodox and biblical doctrines basic to all Christendom, but he also expressed clearly those beliefs which were the distinctives of Roman Catholic doctrine. For example, the saints may intercede for men because of their superadded merit. Grace comes to men through the seven sacraments: baptism, confirmation, the Lord's Supper, extreme unction (at death), penance, ordination, and matrimony. Baptism regenerates man, the Supper builds him up. Private confession must be made to a priest. It is necessary to be subject to the pope. Purgatory is the place of purging for sins of this life. Thomistic philosophical and theological ideas influenced the Roman Catholic church for centuries to come.

Papacy

From the heights of power in the days of Innocent III about 1200, the papacy fell upon hard times in the 1300s and 1400s. The story of the difficulties of the Roman pontiffs in these years is an interesting one but not necessarily illustrative of the power of the Gospel at work in the body of Christ. More often we see a rehearsal of administrative and political power plays and conflicts. Nevertheless, this period is significant to the history of the church in that the pope, even when limited by secular authority, wielded a powerful influence in the church.

In 1309, at the insistence of the king of France, Pope Clement V moved the headquarters of the church from Rome to Avignon on the Rhone River in southern France. For approximately seventy years that city was the headquarters of the church. The French government, while not always able to insure complete control of the policies of the church, nevertheless exerted a strong influence. The move was costly financially, so the papacy embarked upon a program featuring "annates." An annate was the first year's salary of an appointee to high church office. Obviously only the wealthy could afford such a tax, so offices were virtually bought by younger sons of nobility.

With no resident pope, affairs in Rome were in a turmoil. Leaders of Italy urged the popes to return to Rome. Finally in 1377 Pope Gregory XI and his papal court did move back to the city. Gregory died shortly after his return. The citizens of the city pressured the members of the College of Cardinals to choose an Italian, Urban VI, as pope. He was a reformer who demanded that the cardinals change their ways. He also had a strong temper. The cardinals began to have second thoughts about his leadership, claiming the election of Urban invalid because of mob-force. They appointed Clement VII, a relative of the king of France, as pope. Now two popes ruled the church, Urban in Rome, and Clement in Avignon. This was called the Great Schism.

Having more than one claimant to the papal throne was nothing new. At least twenty times before, popes and antipopes had vied with one another for leadership of the church. But this time both popes were appointed by the same College of Cardinals. And more importantly, both popes gathered wide following and support across Europe. France and its allies naturally favored the Avignon papacy; nations opposing France, like England, favored Rome. At the death of the first pope in each of the two lines, new men were selected, to continue the division. Once appointed, no pope was willing to resign his office to produce harmony and unity.

Concerned, church leaders called for a council session to be held in Pisa, Italy to resolve the Great Schism. Hundreds attended the 1409 session. Delegates agreed to depose both popes. A new man, Alexander V, was chosen. The problem was that the two deposed popes refused to recognize the Council of Pisa and refused to resign. Some churchmen now followed each of the three—Rome, Avignon, and the new Pisa-appointed man, so now Europe was even further divided ecclesiastically. The schism was not ended.

Finally, in 1414, another council was held, this time in Constance on the German-Swiss border. Both religious and secular leaders called the session, the most widely attended gathering of the era. This Council was careful that no large groups of people would follow the existing popes. They then deposed two of them and received the resignation of a third. A new man, Martin V, was chosen, who gained the following of the church. The Great Schism was ended.

For a time advocates of the council method of doing church business claimed that the authority of the council was greater than that of the pope. They hoped to broaden the authority base of the church beyond the absolutism of the papacy. Several additional council sessions were held, but their accomplishments were minimal. The papacy, in spite of the problems of Avignon and the Great Schism, maintained its power.

In the 1400s the papacy was influenced strongly by the remarkable outpouring of culture associated with the Renaissance. Popes became enamored with their positions as Italian politicians and patrons of culture. Secular humanists took positions as key advisers to the popes. Some magnificent artistic and cultural work was done, such as the Sistine Chapel and its decoration, but often at the expense of religious life. Innocent VIII, 1484-1492, was dishonest and immoral. He sired sixteen openly acknowledged illegitimate children. His successor, Alexander VI, 1492-1503, bribed eighteen cardinals to gain his office and continued to use dishonest means to administrate it. Julius II, 1503-1513, termed the "warrior pope," was a military genius. Leo X, 1513-1521, of the Medici family from Florence, was principally concerned with art, culture, and luxury. To gain funds to finance the building of the grand St. Peters Cathedral, he advocated the sale of the indulgences and thereby aroused Martin Luther's ire. In short, the Renaissance papacy was secular and corrupt, scarcely the type of leadership which could bring the church back to spiritual moorings.

Preparation for the Reformation

By the 1400s, the church was clearly in need of reform. Doctrinal deviations from biblical norms, problems in the papacy, administrative wrangles all pointed to that need. It would seem that God was providentially preparing the way for successful change in the church as well. The growth of nation states, the Renaissance intellectual stimulus, and some key individuals played a part in that preparation.

The late Middle Ages witnessed the growth of nation states in western Europe and greatly lessened the political influence of the church . Popes were to find it increasingly difficult to enforce their will against strong kings with national support.

France had earlier gained a sense of national unity in the Hundred Years' War against the English. That struggle, which began in 1337, saw the French, inspired by Joan of

Arc, eventually join forces to oust the English king and his feudal holdings from the continent. By 1500, the French government was strong and enjoyed widespread support. In many ways the state controlled the church, checking abuses and making appointments.

England had developed early in its history a sense of national unity. The War of the Roses in the fifteenth century strengthened that unity as the Tudor family, under King Henry VII, emerged from the war in a place of unquestioned leadership.

Spain and Portugal also developed nationally. The long conflicts of these nations against their Muslim overlords were rewarded. The Moors were driven from the last Spanish province in 1492. War with the Moors promoted unity among the Spanish and Portuguese people and caused the Spanish church to remain loyal to traditional Catholicism. Archbishop of Toledo, Cardinal Ximenes, was a zealous leader of strict Catholicism in addition to being the confessor and adviser to Queen Isabella. The Inquisition found its most vigorous expressions in Spain.

To the north, in Germany, there was no national unity. While the Holy Roman Empire provided a governmental structure in theory, in actuality the local princely states held the real power. Is it any wonder that the Reformation thrived in this land where no central force could stop it, rather than in united Spain?

The Renaissance, an intellectual and cultural movement in Europe from about 1300 to 1550, provided some opposition to the church through its secularism. But it also eventually proved helpful to church reform. In northern Europe, Renaissance thinkers were more religious in their frame of thought. While the Renaissance thinkers in Italy stressed study of the ancient classics, the northern Renaissance scholarship turned to the study of biblical manuscripts. The result was a healthy outpouring of biblical scholarship which had not been seen for many years. Johann Reuchlin opened biblical Hebrew to Christian study. Desiderius Erasmus compiled an excellent (for that day) Greek text of the New Testament. He also used a brilliant, satirical pen to attack abuses in the church in his work, *In Praise of Folly*. Englishman, John Colet, emphasized a literal exegesis of the Scriptures as did French scholar Jacques LeFevre. Evidence of spiritual hunger appeared in Europe in these days; the northern Renaissance scholars helped provide a biblical base to answer that hunger.

John Wycliff, 1328?-1384, has been called the "Morning Star of the Reformation." A friend of the king of England, Wycliff attacked abuses within the church, including the doctrine of transubstantiation, the belief in receiving Christ in the elements of the Lord's Supper. He said that if that doctrine were true, ". . .a hog, a dog, or a mouse could eat our Lord." Constructively, Wycliff sponsored the translation of the Bible into Middle English, making the entire Bible available in that language for the first time. He also sent out his followers, the Lollards or "Poor Priests," into the countryside to preach and teach the Bible in English to the people.

John Hus, 1373-1415, learned of Wycliff's ideas and adopted some of them. Adding thoughts of his own, Hus became a leading reformer in Bohemia (western Czechoslovakia today). He was widely accepted and followed, becoming not only a symbol of religious renewal but also of Czech nationalism. The Council of Constance burned him at the stake, in spite of a promise of safe conduct from Emperor Sigismund.

Girolamo Savonarola, 1452-1498, was an Italian monk who preached against the sin and vice of that land. He became the virtual ruler of the city of Florence for a time. Pope Alexander VI, embarrassed by his asceticism, threatened him and then tried to bribe him with the offer of a position as a cardinal. Finally Savonarola was betrayed, tortured, and hanged.

These three pre-reformers are illustrative of the climate for change and reform which existed in Europe by the year 1500. God seemed to be laying a foundation upon which Luther and the other reformers could rebuild. In spite of man's opposition and additions, God would continue to build His church.

6

Building through Reform

Time line   1300   1400   1500   1600   1700

While the building of God's church, the body of Christ, had been slowed during the Middle Ages, the Reformation period saw a dramatic change in the process of spiritual construction. The setting for the Reformation was prepared. Nation states were increasingly independent of the papacy. An aggressive and thoughtful middle class had arisen. Biblical study flourished in some universities. Great spiritual hunger permeated society.

The Protestant movement, led by Luther, Zwingli, Calvin, and others, brought biblical teaching back to the church. Some have called the movement a revolution because of its dramatic changes. The term reformation fits well if we think of it as a re-forming of the church in its New Testament image.

Martin Luther

Martin Luther was born in 1483 into a peasant home in Saxony, Germany. Although his family was poor, he was given opportunity for education in Brethren of the Common Life and other schools. At the University of Erfurt, he completed his bachelor's and master's degrees, demonstrating skill as a scholar. Law was his field of academic interest.

However, Luther sensed a deep spiritual vacuum in his life. When faced with the death of a friend, he realized his need of God. Frightened when caught outside in a storm Luther vowed to St. Anne, a popular saint in Saxony at the time, that he would enter a monastery. He abandoned his law studies in 1505 and entered the cloister of the Augustinian monastery in Erfurt.

In the monastery, Luther was a diligent seeker. He engaged in a vigorous round of religious activities, seeking to please God and find peace. He asked questions, frequently visited the confessional, prayed at length. Later he said of those days, "If I had kept on any longer, I should have killed myself with vigils, prayers, reading, and other work." But he could never balance the ledger. His sin always outweighed the deeds of righteousness and goodness in his life.

His superiors appointed him a teacher at Wittenburg University in an effort to occupy his questioning mind. To encourage his faith, they also sent him on an errand to Rome for the Augustinian order. While in Rome, Luther busily occupied himself with masses and prayers. Rome was supposedly a storehouse of merit. The scissors claimed used to clip John's hair and one of the coins Judas received for betraying Christ were there. So too was the Scala Sancta or sacred staircase, where Christ was supposed to have climbed to Pilate's judgment hall. Far from being a spiritual highlight, the visit to Renaissance Rome raised further doubts. It also shocked the devout German. Italian priests were openly immoral and unbelieving.

Luther's university teaching position in time provided the basis for the answer to his spiritual quest. As a doctor of theology, Luther taught the Bible and theological concepts at Wittenburg. He was a dynamic, popular teacher and preacher who used the original biblical languages in his study. The Word of God opened the truth to him. Romans 1:17, "the just shall live by faith," provided the answer. Luther saw that man did not achieve any righteousness through what he did in self-effort, but only through faith in Jesus Christ. Sometime around 1513, he experienced conversion. He said of the experience, "I felt myself to have been reborn and to have entered the very gates of paradise."

Luther the Reformer

The converted monk pondered his next steps. He could not leave the monastery and find fellowship and theological instruction at the evangelical church on the next corner! He continued, faithfully, to study the Scriptures. Over a period of months, his theology was remolded from medieval Roman patterns into New Testament beliefs.

One event brought Luther to the attention of all Germany. Pope Leo X, in order to build St. Peter's Cathedral in Rome, had proclaimed the sale of indulgences to raise funds. A monk named Tetzel zealously sold these letters of supposed spiritual favor in Germany. When Tetzel arrived in a town, he created a carnival atmosphere, using emotional appeals to the memory of dear, dead loved ones to increase sales. These practices and the total concept of indulgences irritated Luther. In response, in 1517 he wrote his *Ninety-five Theses,* formal statements for debate on the issue. In addition to the scholars for whom they were intended, the *Theses* were read by Germans all over the land. By now the printing press had been perfected, making mass production possible. Overnight, Luther's name was a household word. Many Germans agreed heartily with his stand.

Church leaders reacted to the furor by questioning and challenging Luther. In 1519, he accompanied fellow Wittenburg teacher, Andreas Karlstadt, to a debate with Roman Catholic theologian, John Eck, at Leipzig. There Luther declared that popes and councils can make mistakes. Pope Leo responded by issuing an excommunication decree against Luther. Leo described him as a "wild boar who had invaded the vineyard of the Lord." But Luther, under local protection and assistance, continued his work.

At Worms, in 1521, Luther was called before the parliament of the Holy Roman Empire, presided over by the emperor Charles V. There, before men of rank and wealth, Luther defended his writings and beliefs with courage. His concluding statement at Worms has become a classic:

> "My conscience is captive to the Word of God. I cannot and I will not recant anything, for to go against conscience is neither right nor safe. God help me. Amen."

On the return from Worms, Luther was intercepted by friendly forces and taken to the Wartburg Castle to hide for a time from the imperial troops. While at Wartburg, Luther translated the Bible into German. Although this was not the first German vernacular translation, it was an excellent version in the language of the people. It became the German Bible for centuries, occupying an influential position similar to the King James Version in English.

For some, Luther was too cautious and slow in his reforming program. His colleague Karlstadt, for one, urged more radical action. The resultant upheaval at Wittenburg forced Luther to return to his classroom and pulpit. Wisely, he avoided extreme acts which would have made the reform seem unruly and mob-directed.

When the peasants of south Germany protested unjust social and economic conditions, using some of Luther's ideas as support, Luther opposed their violence and rioting. He favored a well-regulated state with princes in strong control. His conservatism here has been attacked in later years as having promoted tyranny. In his day, however, it undoubtedly saved the Reformation. Had he sided with the peasants, the princes might well have crushed both the uprising and the reform.

A number of associates came to assist Luther in these years. Elector Frederick the Wise, the secular ruler of part of Saxony, protected Luther and presented his cause in official places. Philip Melancthon, a scholar and fellow teacher, contributed to church and theological life. Luther met Katherine von Bora, a former nun, and married her in 1525. Katie, as Martin called her, created a happy home, though it was a very busy one. Numerous strangers, students, visitors, and boarders came to the Luthers' home.

Still German officialdom attempted to restore the unity in the church and state which had been fragmented by the Lutheran movement. Several parliamentary gatherings were held which considered that issue. At Speier in 1529, the Lutheran party presented a "Protestatio" or affirmation of faith to the parliament. Although it was rejected, we take the name Protestant from it. At Augsburg in 1530, a Confession, written largely by Melancthon, was presented. Again it was refused by the empire, but it became the primary doctrinal statement of Lutheranism in the years which followed. Since Luther was under the ban of the empire and could not attend Augsburg, his position was defended there by the princes who had come to his side.

Martin Luther was a powerful personality. Like the rest of us, Luther had his faults and weaknesses. He reflected the coarseness of the fifteenth century German peasantry. He suffered periods of deep depression and anxiety. Yet he presents an appealing image to those who read his works. Luther was outspoken and aggressive. If he put his foot in his mouth, as he could do, he jammed it all the way down! His mistakes were big ones. He could thunder loudly and "name-call" with vigor. Still there was a tender side to this giant too, encouraged and developed by his wife, Katherine.

Theologically, Luther is a watershed figure in church history. His doctrine of justification—that man finds a right relationship with God solely by faith and not by his own works—is the hallmark of Protestantism. He stressed the authority of the Scripture. Disavowing the authority of church fathers, popes, councils, and other tradition, Luther insisted on the Bible as the sole rule of faith and practice. He put great emphasis, as well, upon the concept that life should not be compartmentalized into sacred and secular. The farmer and the milkmaid could find the joy of pleasing God in their daily tasks. The priesthood of all believers, the doctrine that one may approach God directly and not go through a priest as intermediary, expressed this sense of equality in the body of Christ. Luther placed special correlation between Word and sacrament in his theology. Many believers still disagree with Luther's concept that baptism is a regenerative experience for the infant and with his concept of the Lord's Supper. These differences over the sacraments have separated Lutheran and Reformed Protestants through the centuries.

In time it became apparent that Luther's desire to change the church of Rome could not be accomplished. In spite of his intentions to the contrary, a new church body came into being, the Lutheran church. Organizationally, the territorial church principle was prominent. The princes of the various provinces of Germany had a major voice in determining whether the church in their lands would be Roman Catholic or Lutheran. The Lutheran churches would be organized and supervised within each separate province. Schools were organized to teach Protestant doctrine to young people and adults. Biblical preaching was encouraged in each parish. Luther was also a firm advocate of the power of Christian music, so he encouraged the writing of hymns, congregational singing, and other musical expressions.

Luther's pen continued to be a vital weapon in his work. He wrote works against the errors of Catholicism like *The Babylonish Captivity of the Church*, appeals to secular leaders like *To the Christian Nobility of the German Nation*, theological works like *On the Bondage of the Will*, Bible commentaries, and hundreds of sermons.

After Luther's death in 1546, his church continued to gain strength. Nine years later, in 1555, the German parliament finally agreed to tolerate Lutheranism in the states where Lutheran princes ruled. The continuous opposition and occasional outbreaks of warfare, which had occurred the previous twenty years, ended. Much of northern and eastern Germany was, by this time, Lutheran.

Lutheranism Spreads

Students from nearby lands came to Wittenburg to study with Lutheran leaders and returned to their homes to spread the faith. Through the work of Hans Tausen, who translated the New Testament into Danish, and King Christian III, the church in Denmark became Protestant. Since Norway was ruled by the Danes at the time, that land was turned to Lutheranism too. Iceland, also Danish territory then, followed, encouraged and led by former

Wittenburg student, Pastor Einarsen. Sweden was taught by reformer Olaf Petersson, who published the Swedish New Testament. Swedish King Gustaf Vasa encouraged the reformers. Finland was ruled by the Swedes, so followed into the Protestant camp. In East Prussia on the Baltic, Albert, the Grand Master of the religious order which ruled the land, became a Lutheran and brought the land with him. Lutheranism became the official state religion of all these lands.

Even in areas where the majority did not become Protestant, a Lutheran witness spread. Business people in Poland responded to the Protestant message. German-speaking people in Bohemia and Hungary became Lutherans. So did Czech and Magyar speaking people in those lands. It was clear by 1600 that Lutheranism would continue to be a major Christian force.

The Zwinglian Reformation

To the south in Switzerland, a similar reforming movement was occurring in the church at about the same time Luther was doing his work. Switzerland allowed considerable local freedom of expression, making it possible for new ideas to develop and grow.

Huldreich Zwingli came from a government official's home in northeast Switzerland. He received an excellent education in Swiss schools, the Universities of Vienna, Paris, and Basel. He also learned of the importance of a literal study of the Scriptures, rather than the allegorical study common then. Zwingli became a priest and served several parishes in Switzerland.

In 1519, he was called to Zurich, a major Swiss city, to serve a church. In that year he suffered a serious physical malady, which afforded his time for reflection. During this

Building through Reform 73

time he had a significant spiritual experience which changed his life and ministry. His reforming work dates from this conversion.

Zwingli began to preach expository messages through the New Testament. His audiences were thrilled; the church was filled. Gradually the message of the Bible began to grip his thinking about church belief and practice. He moved to change nonbiblical practices to follow Scripture. Eventually he attempted to remove all elements of church life not expressly mentioned in the New Testament. Music was eliminated in much Zwinglian worship. Church buildings were severely simple.

The story of reform in Switzerland has similarities to the Lutheran reform in Germany. Zwingli faced major opposition from Roman Catholic leaders in public confrontations. He opposed those he thought too radical. His movement spread to neighboring Swiss cities and cantons (provinces). Through preaching, teaching, and writing, the leaders of the movement attempted to train the people in the faith.

It is significant that without major interaction, Zwingli and Luther would arrive at very similar positions of reform at the same time. It appeared to German prince, Philip of Hesse, that it would be good if the two movements could be brought together. As a result, a conference was held at Marburg in 1529 to attempt unity. Luther and Zwingli agreed on most major doctrinal issues. They came into sharp conflict, however, over the doctrine of the Lord's Supper. Luther insisted that Christ was present "in, with, and under" the elements of communion in a special way He is not present elsewhere. This position came to be called **Consubstantiation**. Zwingli believed that the elements of communion were but signs or symbols of the body and blood of Christ and held no special sense of Christ's presence in themselves. The two could not agree. Their churches remained divided.

Governments of the Roman Catholic provinces in Switzerland strongly opposed Zwingli's reform, so much so that warfare broke out between Zwinglian and Catholic groups. In 1531 Zwingli, serving as chaplain to the forces in battle, was killed on the battlefield in the Second Kappel War.

However, the Zwinglian movement was not ended. His son-in-law, Henry Bullinger, continued the reforming work in Switzerland. Zwinglian ideas spread to southwest Germany and to the west into French-speaking Switzerland. (Zwingli's work had been in German-speaking Switzerland previously.) In future years the Zwinglian churches were united with those led by John Calvin to form the Swiss Reformed church, which exists yet today. Zwingli, though often neglected by students of history, was one of the founding fathers of the entire Reformed church movement of church history. Through his work, too, God was building His church.

The Reformation marked a major turning point in the erection of God's church. The Word of God, again made available to the people, was the principal tool of construction.

7

Building with Reforming Zeal

Time line   1300   1400   1500   1600

The work of building the church through reform, begun by Martin Luther, was carried out by other people and movements as well. In this chapter we shall observe how that work was done by the Calvinist, Anabaptist, and Anglican branches of the reform.

The Calvinistic Reformation

About the same time that Luther and Zwingli were discovering the truths of the reformation, earnest men in France were also finding them. Although biblical studies had been done, translation accomplished, and administrative reform attempted in the archbishopric of Meaux, the French reform movement lacked a leader, a central focus. John Calvin was to provide it.

Calvin was born into a middle-class home in northern France in 1509. He was afforded the best education available in the day, including the study of law, theology, and the new humanistic studies of the Renaissance. But the scholarly Calvin, between 1528 and 1534, experienced a sudden conversion to Christ which he later said "tamed my heart and made it teachable."

The following years in Calvin's life provide only sketchy information but an exciting story. He began to associate with other church reformers, fled from Paris under pressure, broke openly with the church, was imprisoned, and finally fled from France in disguise. Although Calvin's personality was shy and perhaps aloof, he was not lacking in courage!

In 1535 he arrived as an exile in Basel, Switzerland, a city of safety and tolerance. In that congenial environment, Calvin began work on his monumental systematic theology work, *The Institutes of the Christian Religion*. It was a masterful piece of French prose, a work which was to be the most significant Protestant theological work of the entire Reformation.

Calvin in his *Institutes* and throughout his ministry, placed great doctrinal emphasis upon the sovereignty of God and obedience to His will. He returned to the theological thrusts of Augustine of the ancient church. The mnemonic device "TULIP" has often been used to summarize Calvin's theology.

T - The "T" stands for Total depravity, or the belief that fallen man's depravity is so extensive that he can do nothing, even believe on his own, to gain God's favor.

U - The "U" represents Unconditional election, the belief that God's choice of those to be saved and damned is not conditioned on anything—man's actions, God's foreknowledge, or anything else.

L - The "L" stands for Limited atonement, that is, Christ's atoning work was limited to the elect.

I - The "I" represents Irresistible grace, or the belief that those whom God has elected will not resist to damnation the grace of God.

P - The "P" indicates Perseverance of the saints, the belief that the elect will persevere unto final salvation and will not totally fall away from grace.

While Calvin was completing this monumental work, a French colleague, Farel, was evangelizing in the Geneva, Switzerland area and receiving tremendous response. When Calvin visited Geneva, Farel demanded on God's authority that Calvin stay in Geneva and organize the new believers. Calvin agreed. For most of the rest of his life Calvin worked in Geneva, attempting to make that city a model Christian community. He taught, wrote Bible commentaries, organized the church, and encouraged industry. The Geneva church came to feature strong biblical preaching and the singing of the Psalms in worship.

Not everyone in Geneva agreed with the changes brought by the Reformation. Old-line Geneva families disliked the foreign leadership. Theologians disagreed with some of Calvin's doctrine. In the face of opposition, John Calvin maintained a rigorous discipline.

His most famous opponent was the Spaniard Michael Servetus. Servetus, under the name Villeneuve, had achieved some remarkable scientific accomplishments. However, he was a unitarian, that is, he denied the full deity of Jesus Christ. When Servetus came to Geneva, he was arrested for heresy, tried, and condemned to death. The execution has become a storm center in the career of Calvin. It should be remembered, however, that Calvin was operating from fifteenth not twentieth century perspectives. Everyone, Roman Catholic and Protestant alike, believed in harsh penalties for unitarianism then. Calvin did not rise above his culture in this respect.

John Calvin worked hard throughout his life. At the close of his life he was troubled by the controversies in Geneva and frail in health. Calvin died in 1564.

The Calvinistic movement spread widely. Geneva-trained pastors returned to build a strong Reformed church in France. Some were persecuted but the church grew and developed. Calvin's teachings became the dominant Protestant position in the Low Countries as well. Numerous Dutch Reformed churches were established.

Scotland became a principal center of Calvinistic Protestantism. Some reformed beginnings were made there through the preaching of Hamilton and Wishart, both of whom were burned at the stake for their faith. John Knox, 1513-1572, however, became the outstanding leader. Accused of conspiracy in the murder of a Roman Catholic bishop, Knox was arrested and spent nineteen months as a galley slave on a French man-of-war. Upon his release, he spent some time studying in Geneva under Calvin before returning to Scotland. Reformation spirit was growing. A group of Scottish noblemen lent their support.

The ruler of Scotland, however, Mary, Queen of Scots, adamantly opposed. Open warfare broke out. Mary's position was weakened markedly when the public saw her as guilty of the murder of her husband, Darnley. She married a nobleman, Bothwell, shortly after the murder, a union which didn't help her reputation either. Eventually she was forced to abdicate the throne. She fled to England, where she was later executed.

Protestantism triumphed fully in Scotland after Mary's departure. Knox was the nation's leading theologian and church organizer. The Scottish church was Calvinistic or reformed and has been termed Presbyterian to this day.

John Calvin's followers also made an impact in Hungary and even briefly in northern Italy. Their influence reached England through the Puritan movement, which we will consider in the next chapter, and from there came to America. Churches today which bear the name Presbyterian, Reformed, or Congregational are Calvin's descendants. Other groups have been strongly influenced by his work.

The Anabaptist Reformation

One of the most misunderstood of Christian groups, the Anabaptists, also developed in the Reformation to become an important part of the building which is God's church. It has been popular in some quarters to ascribe a place to the Anabaptists in an independent, evangelical line of apostolic succession, going back through the Montanists, Waldensians, and other separatist groups. This concept is not good history. Little evidence can be found linking the Anabaptists to medieval groups. Nor is it good theology. We needn't find historical links to independent groups to validate their theology.

The Anabaptist movement is, rather, an offspring of the Reformation. In Zurich, Switzerland, Conrad Grebel and Felix Manz, among others, came to believe that the Zwinglian reform was not going far enough. Both men were well-trained scholars, who advocated a complete biblical practice. The heart of the debate was over the baptism of infants which Grebel and Manz refused as unbiblical. In January of 1525 in Manz's home, Grebel officiated at the first public adult baptism. It created a furor. Enemies called these folk "Anabaptists" or rebaptizers. It was a term of derision denied by the Anabaptists, who did not see infant sprinkling as baptism at all. Persecution broke out and Manz was killed by drowning. It was prophetic of what was to come. Apparently the officials believed that if these folk wanted more water, that was exactly what they would get!

But persecution did not stop the movement. It spread into southern Germany, western Austria, and Moravia (modern Czechoslovakia). Balthasar Hubmaier became its spokesman for a time, uniting, encouraging, and teaching the people. He was burned at the stake in 1528. In fact, all of the early important leaders met death shortly after the inception of the movement. These men had provided an educated, middle class direction to Anabaptism. The leaders who surfaced after persecution were not well trained and the movement suffered as a result.

Under the influence of ignorant preaching, many Anabaptists came to believe that Christ would return to the northwest German city of Munster in the year 1534. Eagerly they flocked to that city. Unscrupulous leadership took over and turned the city into a so-called Reign of Saints. It was anything but that. The leaders were the worst sort of opportunists. The ousted Roman Catholic bishop of that city raised an army against the "Saints" and laid seige to the city. Hunger, starvation, polygamy, immorality, and tyranny were common in Munster until the city finally fell.

This type of fanaticism had been the practice of a minority of professing Anabaptists. Most were quiet, peaceable farm folk. However, governmental authorities, fearing a repetition of the Munster episode, and unable to tell fanatic from quietist, turned the full brunt of persecution on the movement. The Anabaptists were hounded until their church was in danger of complete collapse.

A haven for members of this persecuted group opened in the Netherlands. Menno Simons, 1492-1561, became the leader who stayed the hand of collapse. Menno had been a priest of the Roman church, but was converted and identified with these hunted folk. His warm zeal and wisdom provided the organization, sound theology, and church leadership which the Anabaptists needed. Many Dutch and German Anabaptists, desiring a new identity after Munster, and grateful for Menno's leadership, adopted his name for their movement. From this point they were called Mennonites.

The Anabaptists were not as interested in formal theological statements as they were in living the Christian life. Nevertheless, the movement produced significant contributions to church history in theology and church life. The Schleitheim Confession of 1527 was a notable document illustrating early Anabaptist beliefs.

Baptism of believers upon declaration of faith rather than infants was a hallmark of their position. The mode of baptism was not as significant; some immersed, others poured. The candidate's salvation was the important thing. Because at that time baptism was not only a rite denoting introduction of the infant into the church but also a civic rite showing citizenship somewhat like a birth certificate, Anabaptists were widely and vigorously opposed for this stand. They believed in a regenerate church membership or the concept of the "gathered" church. They did not accept the church as consisting of all members of the community, Christians or not. Voluntarism was basic to their position. Therefore, the church and the state were to be entirely separate. All sects were to be freely tolerated. In these views, too, they ran counter to prevailing Roman Catholic and Protestant practice.

In the governing of the church, persecution forced a

stress upon local autonomy. When it was possible, however, Anabaptists formed associations beyond the local level. Strict discipline was enforced, even to the point of "banning" wayward members who fell into open sin, were divisive, or taught false doctrine.

Hubmaier and other early leaders believed that the Christian should serve in government if he could. Many Anabaptists came to believe that such service was wrong and that a believer should follow a more humble calling. The government leader might be called upon to take a human life; this they could not do. The Anabaptists came to oppose taking civic oaths and bearing of arms. The majority were pacifists. In many cases, they gave up their lives in times of persecution with little or no opposition. They lived their lives as simple farmers. Their worship patterns were also simple and plain.

In other areas of doctrine and practice, Anabaptists followed orthodox, Protestant beliefs. They stressed the authority of the Scriptures, justification by faith, discipleship, and fellowship. They believed that they were going back to New Testament practice.

Their influence has been widespread. In addition to their direct descendants, the Mennonites, they have shaped the ideas held by other evangelical Christian groups. They were 200 years ahead of their time in advocating our American practice of separation of church and state. The question has often been raised, "What about the Baptists?" "Are they Anabaptists?" The Baptists, who were English, were influenced by Dutch Mennonites as we shall see in the next chapter. Therefore the Anabaptists do share in the heritage of that prominent denomination.

The Anglican Reformation

England was another important site of the rebuilding of God's church we know as the Reformation. Reforming influences had been present since the time of John Wycliff in the fourteenth century. His Bible reading emphasis was by no means dead by 1500. Renaissance biblical scholarship had touched the universities. William Tyndale's translation of the Bible had received wide interest and support. English nationalism created a spirit of independence against papal influence. Luther's writings circulated in the country. For these reasons, reform of the church was gradually taking place across the countryside.

The part played by the monarchy, however, heightened the reforming process. England was ruled from 1485 to 1603 by the Tudor family. The founder of the line, Henry VII, brought peace to the kingdom, encouraged trade, and built the royal treasury. He also made a marriage pact allying England with Spain by uniting his son Arthur with Catherine of Aragon, a Spanish princess. At Arthur's untimely death, younger son, Henry VIII, married Catherine, to continue the alliance. This kind of matrimonial diplomacy was common in that period.

Henry VIII, by now the king of England, became dissatisfied with Catherine. Because she had borne him only a daughter and no male heir to continue the Tudor line, he sought from the pope an annulment of the marriage. The pope had previously granted Henry the title "Defender of the Faith" for his staunch Roman Catholic position. He would like to have granted the annulment request, but it would have been unwise for him, politically, to offend Spain in so doing. So he stalled and did not act.

When Henry could not get the papacy to assist him, he pushed through the English Parliament the annulment permission he couldn't get from the pope. Henry married his chambermaid, Anne Boleyn, who bore him another daughter. Parliament passed the Supremacy Act of 1534 which made the king, Henry, not the pope the head of the English church. The government took over the valuable church and monastic lands throughout England. England's break, at this point, with Rome was not based upon biblical or theological issues. It was an administrative conflict. In Henry's lifetime, the doctrine of the separated English church remained largely Roman Catholic with the exception of the now-repudiated doctrine of the papacy.

When Henry tired of Anne Boleyn, she was accused of adultery and beheaded. Eleven days later he married Jane Seymour, who bore him the long-awaited son. After her death, Henry married three other wives in succession. At his death in 1547, the English church was following a middle way, neither fully Protestant nor Roman Catholic.

Henry VIII's successor was his only son, Edward VI, the son of Jane Seymour. Because of his heritage and because of his adviser's beliefs, the reign of Edward, 1547-1553, witnessed a "Protestantizing" of the English church. Theologian Thomas Cranmer encouraged English-language preaching and singing in worship. A theological statement of Protestant content was issued. The still-used Anglican Book of Common Prayer, or worship-form book, was written. But Edward was not strong physically, and died while still young.

His successor was Mary, the daughter of Catherine of Aragon, who ruled 1553-1558. Mary was loyal to her mother's memory and Roman Catholic religion. She and her advisers undid the religious changes which had been accomplished in the two previous reigns. Ties with Rome were again officially reinstated. Protestants were persecuted, some burned at the stake. History has termed her "Bloody Mary" for this period of oppression.

Elizabeth I, 1558-1603, followed her sister. Elizabeth was the daughter of Anne Boleyn and therefore had to insist upon a policy of breaking with Rome if she wanted to be the queen. (The Catholics, of course, considered her illegitimate.) And Elizabeth wanted to be the queen! The Supremacy Act of 1559 again broke ties with Rome, making the queen the supreme governess of the church. The Prayer Book of Edward's day was reissued. A revision of his theological statement, the Thirty-Nine Articles, was adopted. It has been the basic creed of Anglicanism ever since.

During the religious shifts of the earlier rulers, change was often effected largely at the top. But the local parish and common churchman often scarcely felt the changes. They came rapidly and were reversed just as rapidly. Elizabeth ruled long enough, however, for the Church of England, or Anglican church, to develop quite thoroughly in a "middle way" pattern.

The church had elements of both Roman and Protestant leadership and practice. For example, Matthew Parker was consecrated Archbishop of Canterbury in apostolic succession. The Anglicans claimed that Rome had forfeited that position and that they now represented the true succession from the apostles. On the other hand, Bibles were printed and widely distributed, thus sifting ideas down to the people. The Thirty-Nine Articles was a doctrinal statement of sufficient breadth to allow wide variation within its boundaries. Except for a handful of statements, most evangelicals today could affirm its tenets. Church life was characterized by formal, elaborate worship patterns, perhaps in part to compensate for weak preaching from clergy who had "grown up" with the system and not been actively involved in creating it.

The Church of England, or Anglican church, was indeed a broad, middle way, with room for many within its nationalistic structure. It has spread throughout the world, including the United States, where the Episcopal church continues its traditions. Within Anglicanism at the time of the Reformation were those who, in their adherance to the Word of God, assisted in the building of God's church.

Calvinism, Anabaptism, and Anglicanism, in their zeal for the reform of the church, each added its part in this crucial period in the building of God's church.

8

Building in War and Opposition

Time line   1400   1500   **1600**   1700   1800

The years following the initial phases of the Reformation were years of opposition to the reform in a renewed and revitalized Roman Catholicism. These years also witnessed the struggles of intense religious warfare in four areas of Europe. The church, God's building, weathered severe storms but continued to proclaim biblical truth.

The Catholic Reformation

It appeared, in about 1540, that the Roman Catholic church would disintegrate completely. Germany, Scandinavia, Switzerland, the Netherlands, England, and Scotland were being influenced strongly by Protestantism. France was leaning that way too. Even the heartlands of the ancient faith, Italy and Spain, were seeing some Protestant teaching. But Rome rebounded and by the end of the century was able to consolidate its control over many European lands. This we call the Catholic, or Counter-Reformation.

The European peasantry was partially responsible for

this Roman renewal in that many had remained loyal to Catholicism throughout the Reformation. Italian Renaissance scholars, strongly disliking Protestant theology, gave intellectual support to Rome. Spain, long accustomed to crusading against the Moors, now led in a crusade against Protestants. Emperors Charles V and Philip II of Spain devoted large sums of money, some of it raised from Spain's new colonies in the New World, to the putting down of heresy. Spanish armies fought to retake areas lost to the church. The Spanish Inquisition was exported to other nations.

Three specific church activities were central to the Catholic reformation: the Council of Trent, the Jesuit order, and papal reform. In the past, the church had often dealt with problems by calling councils to consider them. To Trent, in northern Italy, 1545-1563, Roman Catholic leaders came for a council to deal with the problems of their era. No Protestants were invited. Trent clearly upheld the traditional, medieval doctrines of the Roman church, making no concessions to Protestant theology. Now persons on the fence had to make a definite choice; no longer could they remain indecisive. Trent also activated a policy of listing an Index of prohibited books for the faithful. Protestant writings and biblical translations were included on the list. Some elements of internal reform of church practice were considered, but not much was accomplished. Trent represents a decisiveness and revitalization of Catholicism.

Several new religious orders were begun in the Catholic reformation era, none more important than the Jesuit order or the Society of Jesus. The mystic, Ignatius Loyola, founded that society, which professed to carry chivalry and military obedience into the church. Loyola was devout and well educated. His *Spiritual Exercises* was a highly influential writing on Catholic piety. The Jesuits traveled across Europe opposing Protestantism, teaching, and preaching. Eventually they served as missionaries all over the world. Many schools and universities were founded by the order.

The corruption and secularism of the papacy of the Renaissance was brought to a halt in the Catholic reformation era. Men of integrity and Catholic piety were elected popes. They then in turn used their influence to demand piety and obedience from the curia (papal administration) and the cardinalate. Cardinal Caraffa, who became Pope Paul IV, 1555-1559, was one of the leading men of this period. Through vigorous use of the Inquisition and thorough reform of the papacy itself, Caraffa advanced the Roman cause effectively. Other popes who followed added respect and strength to the office. From the Catholic reformation on, the papacy never again sank to the low levels of immorality and corruption of previous years. It was usually typified by men of integrity and Catholic devotion.

The rebounding of the Roman church meant that Christendom would no longer be plagued by corrupt and immoral leadership. However, it also meant increased difficulty for the expansion and growth of biblical teaching and truth.

The Continental Wars of Religion

The Netherlands was the scene of considerable growth of Protestant groups—Mennonite and Reformed particularly. But the Netherlands was governed by the devoutly-Catholic Spanish. Inevitably, the two came into conflict.

Emperor Philip II of Spain was determined to crush heresy everywhere, including his Dutch possessions. The

Dutch in this period were increasingly nationalistic, resentful of Spanish domination politically. Thus, Dutch Protestantism came to be allied with Dutch nationalism in the quest to oust the Spanish from the land. A War for Independence broke out with the rebels, led by nobleman William of Orange, contending against the Spanish army. Eventually, after a bitter struggle, the northern part of the Low Countries was successful in throwing off the Spanish yoke. Spain retained control of the south, modern Belgium.

During this period of struggle, the Dutch Reformed church emerged as the dominant religious body of the north. Its theology was staunchly Calvinistic, its church order presbyterian or representative in form. The land came to be quite tolerant, however, of varying religious opinions. In the struggle against Spain, men of all parties were needed for victory. This spirit continued after the war. In 1577 Anabaptist-Mennonites were given the first official protection in worship in the Netherlands.

However the Dutch Reformed church experienced division within its own ranks in these years. James Arminius was a theological professor at the University of Leyden. In the course of his studies there, he came to have personal doubts concerning the Calvinistic doctrine of God's decrees of election. Arminius began to teach a greater role for the responsibility of man in salvation than the Calvinistic system accorded.

His teaching created a furor. Arminius had touched the vital nerve of Calvinism. His followers, the Remonstrants, were ousted from the church. His teaching, which we term Arminianism, has continued and has been modified throughout subsequent history.

In France, as well, conflict developed. The French Calvinists, termed Huguenots, greatly increased their strength throughout the 1540s and 50s. Politically, they were often allied with a party which stressed local authority. The monarchy, naturally, wished to see the central government strengthened, so used the Roman Catholic church as an agency. Catherine de Medici, the mother of three weak and short-lived kings in the period, actually dominated the government.

When some Protestants who were worshipping in a barn at Vassy were killed, warfare broke out. A series of eight dreary wars with intermittent truces devastated France. These were termed the Huguenot Wars. The infamous St. Bartholomew's Day massacre in 1572 at which several thousand Protestants were killed was a part of this era.

Finally a secular party arose which came to believe that the wars were helping neither Protestants nor Catholics. The political elements involved in the struggle were not gaining either. The only result seemed to be the ruin of France. By an unusual train of circumstances, a Protestant leader, Henry of Navarre, came to be the heir to the French throne. In order to be crowned king, Henry turned Catholic. When he became King Henry IV, peace was proclaimed. He issued the Edict of Nantes in 1598 granting official, legal toleration to the Huguenots in France. It was a remarkale document which took into account the welfare of the religious groups and also the nation as a whole.

The one hundred years which followed were the period of greatest Protestant strength in France. Churches and schools flourished. In 1685 King Louis XIV revoked the toleration policy and again attacked Protestants, creating the situation of spiritual weakness which still exists in France.

Germany was the site of the most devastating of the religious wars of this era, the Thirty Years War. The latter half of the 1500s were years of Lutheran growth and development, in spite of theological controversy and a lack of warmth in some parts of that church. The *Formula of Concord* of 1577 is a notable creedal statement coming from this period. The Calvinists, also, grew in strength.

Conflict broke out in 1618 between the growing Protestant forces and the entrenched Catholic leadership. As in the Netherlands and France, it would be unfair to ascribe the warfare just to religious positions. Political considerations were an important part of the struggle. The questions of local authority vs. central government, the power of the Hapsburg family, and personal ambition surfaced often.

War ravaged the German countryside. The Bohemians and Danes were involved. The Spaniards fought. King Gustavus Adolphus of Sweden brought an army to Germany and assisted Protestant forces in northern Germany. Catholic France fought against the Catholic Hapsburg forces, a good illustration of the decline of religion as a factor in the later years of the war.

Finally in 1648, the Thirty Years War was concluded in the Peace of Westphalia. Boundaries between Catholic and Protestant were fixed again. However, the war had been terribly hard on the vitality of Christianity. Hatred filled men's hearts in the wake of the heavy loss of life. Study and regular worship were interrupted as towns were destroyed. Morals were lowered as armies marched back and forth across the land. It was not a period of much solid building of the church of God.

English War of Religion

Warfare, with religious overtones, touched England too. The story of the Spanish Armada of 1588 is perhaps the best known example. The Armada was an attempt to strengthen Spanish national interests in the north Atlantic, but it also had a zealous, crusading thrust aimed at putting down the Protestant heresy. The defeat of the Armada launched England on her path to greatness; it also strengthened Protestant elements within that land.

Conflict also broke out within the Anglican-Protestant community itself. We have seen the emphasis within the Church of England upon a broad, middle-way approach to Christianity. Zealous Protestants, many of them influenced by Calvinistic teaching and contacts on the continent, were dissatisfied with this. Because they were determined to purify the Anglican church of its Roman Catholic elements, they came to be known as the Puritan party. Although the Puritans varied widely, they were unified in their attack on specific practices in the church. They favored a robe more simple than the elaborate vestments worn by the clergy. (Remember that the twentieth century American business suit was not worn in the pulpit then!) They opposed saints' days and formal practices in the Lord's Supper. They disliked the hierarchy organization of the church, many favoring a presbyterian or representative system of church government. The Puritans were a strong element within the church and almost persuaded parliament to pass laws favorable to their cause.

At the death of Queen Elizabeth I in 1603, the crown passed to a new family line, the Stuarts, and to King James I from Scotland, who ruled from 1603 to 1625. Roman Catholic extremists, reacting to the banishment of priests from England, embarrassed their fellow religionists by a fantastic plot to blow up the king, cabinet, and parliament. Its discovery and the subsequent execution of the plotters brought discredit to the entire Roman position.

Puritans also pressed their position, urging James to adopt further reform. But James favored the middle-way approach which had been a hallmark of Anglicanism since the beginning. He would bend neither to Catholic nor Puritan pressure. The one result of Puritan agitation in these years was the publication of a new English Bible translation in 1611. This authorized King James Version was vigorously opposed at first, but came to hold a position of dominance in the English-speaking world for 350 years.

New opinions and groups were surfacing in the era of James I. Some Puritans wanted to change the Church of England not to presbyterian forms, but to congregational. That is, they believed in a state church, but wanted it to be organized so that the local congregation held the authority. Henry Jacob led this group, termed independents. They founded a church in 1616 which is thought to be the first congregational church which survived.

Others, who held to a congregational church polity, believed that it could never be implemented in a state church system. These separatists, as they came to be called, led by Brown, Barrow, and others, believed in forming groups which had no tie at all to the Church of England. They were persecuted vigorously; some fled to the Netherlands, later to come to America on board the Mayflower.

While in the Netherlands, a group of separatists came into contact with the Mennonites and became convinced of the doctrine of believers' baptism. Under the leadership of John Smyth and Thomas Helwys, they formed a baptistic group. When some of them returned to England, they founded the first Baptist church in England in 1611.

James I was succeeded by his son, Charles I, who ruled from 1625 to 1649. Stubborn and autocratic, Charles enforced a firm religious policy upon the nation. His adviser, William Laud, harassed the Puritans, driving many of them to New England. Charles also alienated many Englishmen politically, particularly a strong pro-parliament party which opposed him.

The result was the English Civil War. On one side were the Puritan-parlimentary forces, called the roundheads because of their haircut style. On the other were the Anglican-monarchy forces, called Cavaliers. The Scots were involved in the war as well, fighting on the parliamentary side.

For a time, during a conflict, it seemed as if Presbyterianism would be the victorious religious position. An assembly met which drew up the famous Westminster Confession and Catechism, documents which became the theological statement of Presbyterianism the world around. The Independents, however, came to occupy a strong position within the army.

Finally, the parliamentary forces triumphed. King Charles I was executed. General Oliver Cromwell became the Protector, or virtual dictator, of England. During the period of 1649 to 1660 when there was no king, a broad policy of religious toleration was instituted for all Protestant groups. Also begun, was a program of moral strictness.

A new group was born in the Cromwellian era, the Society of Friends, or the Quakers. George Fox was the founder of this group, which stressed the "inner light" within man leading him to God and a full equality of believers. They opposed the sacraments, a paid clergy, and warfare. They were persecuted severly in England and many came to the New World to find religious freedom.

In 1660, England, tired of the upheavals of the Cromwell era, brought back the Stuarts in the person of King Charles II, 1660-1685. They also brought back parliament and the Anglican Church. In reaction against Puritanism, strict laws were again passed enforcing Anglican conformity. The country also embarked on a wave of loose conduct, led by a king whose personal life was thoroughly immoral. Charles secretly favored the Roman Catholic position and was baptized a Catholic on his deathbed.

His brother, James II, 1685-1688, who followed him, was an avowed Catholic. He encouraged the Roman position in government policy and ignored parliamentary legislation. When a son was born to the king, seemingly indicating continued Roman Catholic rule, parliamentary leaders ousted James in what has been termed the Glorious Revolution. James' Protestant daughter Mary and her husband William of Orange (the grandson of the William studied in the previous section) were invited to become the joint sovereigns of England. The rule of William and Mary has tremendous implications for the concept of parlimentary democracy for England. It also has significance religiously in that it results in the final triumph of Protestantism.

In 1689 the English Toleration Act was passed, giving religious toleration to Protestant dissenters. From this point on, persecution would no longer hinder the progress of the Gospel in England.

This period of religious struggle in England produced rich literary heritage for Protestantism. Writers John Bunyan (*Pilgrim's Progress*) and John Milton (*Paradise Lost*) have exerted great influence through their pens. Devotional writer William Law's *Serious Call to a Devout and Holy Life* stirred men's attention. Hymn writer Isaac Watts became the virtual creator of the English hymn. We still sing his "When I Survey the Wondrous Cross," "Joy to the World," "O God Our Help in Ages Past," and "Jesus Shall Reign."

In spite of opposition and the violence of war, God continued in the late 1500s and the 1600s to build His church. The building process which was being done in those years influenced not only Europe, but was to have great significance in shaping the early years of America as well.

9

Building in Revival

Time line   1500   1600   1700   1800   1900

The vitality of the Christian church contrastingly ebbed and flowed in the years following the religious wars. Strong rationalism reacted against traditional Protestant orthodoxy and its doctrinal standards. At the same time a vigorous revivalism, or pietism, reacted against the lack of warmth and personal experience in the church. In spite of the rationalistic trends, God built His church, often through great revival movements.

Opposition to Christianity

The world of the seventeenth and eighteenth centuries was changing intellectually. Men of science—Bacon, Galileo, and Newton—were demonstrating the regularity of the universe and explaining its operation according to specific natural law. Men of philosophy such as Descartes and Spinoza were questioning traditional knowledge and emphasizing man's reason. To some, these intellectual developments challenged Christian values including the very belief in God Himself.

As man became more and more enamored of his own capabilities, his view of God faded into the background. A new concept of the Supreme Being, which we term deism, developed. To the deist, God was like a great clock maker who set in motion the processes of the universe. The processes followed unchanging laws without God's involvement. Plainly He was not directly active in creation, salvation, or men's lives.

Some deists maintained semi-Christian terminology and ties; others repudiated any connection. Deistic writers made a profound impact upon the intellectual communities of Europe. Englishmen John Toland, Matthew Tindal, and David Hume wrote and taught deistic ideologies. On the continent, the terms "Age of Enlightenment" or "Age of Reason" have come to be associated with deistic thought. Frenchmen Voltaire probably is the best known exponent of enlightenment views.

Deism made considerable impact upon the intellectuals of early America. Thomas Paine, the publicist of the American Revolution, patriot Benjamin Franklin, and Thomas Jefferson, author of the Declaration of Independence and third President of the United States, were of deistic persuasion. Deistic terminology and thought patterns appear in the documents of the revolutionary period. Not all the founding fathers of United States history were strongly Christian; many were deists, who opposed Christian truth.

The upper classes of Russia drifted from Russian Orthodoxy in these years. Roman Catholicism in Austria was affected. In France the ideology of the French Revolution clearly incorporated deistic thought.

Unitarianism developed as an organized religious group out of this climate of opinion. Although the denial of the full deity of Jesus Christ has challenged the church from its beginnings, in the eighteenth century the idea developed into a fully organized group. In 1774, Englishmen established the first Unitarian church in London. Joseph Priestley, a former Presbyterian clergyman, encouraged Unitarian opinion in both England and the United States. Unitarianism remains a thoroughly liberal religious organization today, exerting an influence out of proportion to its limited membership size.

In Germany, too, Enlightenment and anti-Christian thought came to the fore. Scholars such as Wolff, von Mosheim, Reimarus, Lessing, and Eichhorn challenged biblical patterns. They and men like them laid the foundations for the long-standing German intellectual challenges to Christian orthodoxy.

The Wesleyan Movement

But God could not be content with defection and defeat. He called out men and a movement to champion His cause.

The England of the 1700s was troubled, not only with intellectuals who opposed the faith, but also by widesread spiritual lethargy, disinterest, neglect, and immorality among the people. Here and there signs appeared of a spiritual stirring. In Scotland and Wales successful evangelism brought men to Christ. Still the great masses were untouched.

The life and ministry of John Wesley brought the message of the Gospel to England in a powerful way. Wesley was born into a poor, Anglican church parsonage in 1703, the fifteenth of seventeen children. A bright lad, he was eager for all the education he could get.

At seventeen, he entered Oxford University, where he excelled. John and his brother, Charles, became the leaders of a group of men who desired to live upright lives in the face of the corruption of the day at Oxford. This so-called Holy Club devoted itself to the study of devotional works and to living methodical lives. They were, thus, given the name "Methodists."

Desiring to extend their field of service, John and Charles Wesley sailed to the rough frontier colony of Georgia in 1735 as missionaries. Here John began to realize the futility of trying to do God's work in his own strength. He embarked on a program of strict, high-church Anglicanism which didn't fit the frontier. It only demonstrated further his own spiritual emptiness.

The tragedy of Wesley's condition and his unregenerate state is seen clearly in his journal entry for January 24, 1738: "I went to America to convert the Indians; but O, who shall convert me?" Some Moravians assisted him in his personal spiritual quest. Finally, having returned to England, Wesley attended an Anglican service on Aldersgate Street in May of 1738. The Preface to Luther's *Commentary on Romans* was being read. The self-righteous preacher opened his heart personally to Jesus Christ. He said, "I felt my heart strangely warmed."

The significant aspect of the Aldersgate Street experience is that it changed John Wesley's life. He began to preach vigorously a Gospel of grace and faith. So outspoken did he become, that many Anglican pulpits throughout the land were closed to him. The result was that Wesley began to preach outdoors. The thought of such a thing horrified proper Englishmen. They thought it virtually a sin to save a man outside a church building! But "field preaching," as it came to be called, became a hallmark of Wesley's ministry. "The world is my parish" became his slogan.

The neglected areas of England heard the Gospel message—newly developed cities and larger towns with crowded and dingy streets and homes, rural areas, and small towns. The responses were overwhelming. Great emotional waves of hysteria swept over his audiences, causing Wesley great concern in controlling the crowds. Fierce persecution was his lot on other occasions. The results were undeniable: thousands were won to faith in Jesus Christ.

From the beginning, the methodical Wesley was determined to organize these raw converts in order to preserve the fruit of evangelism. They were gathered into classes of about a dozen, led by a local layman. The classes of a given area were united into Methodist Societies, also generally lay-led. Circuit-riding preachers visited the societies as often as they could to teach and train the believers. Annual conferences were held for the entire movement. Simple, austere buildings were erected for worship and study. John Wesley himself oversaw the entire procedure, controlling the Methodist movement until his death.

Wesley emphasized Christian experience, rather than any formal creedal doctrinal position. He taught the great doctrines of Protestant orthodoxy, interpreting them from an Arminian perspective. His great stress was upon the new birth, the change God makes in the life of the believer. He also taught the distinctive Wesleyan view, "Christian perfection," his approach to the doctrine of sanctification. To Wesley, this perfection consisted in a heart of perfect love toward God. The emphasis upon Christian experience was surely healthy.

One of John Wesley's key associates was the powerful evangelist George Whitefield. Perhaps one of the most gifted speakers the church has ever known, Whitefield preached in both England and America. So powerful was his delivery that a listening actor once remarked, "That man could say 'Mesopotamia' and the crowds would weep." Whitefield was a Calvinist, who at times disagreed theologically with Wesley. At other times, they put these differences aside and worked harmoniously together.

John's brother, Charles, was another key associate in the work. Charles not only preached and organized but was also the hymn writer of the Wesleyan movement. Singing was an important part of Methodist church life. They sang the message of the Gospel across England. We still use some of Charles Wesley's hymns: "O for a Thousand Tongues to Sing," "Jesus Lover of My Soul," "Love Divine, All Loves Excelling," and others.

As long as John Wesley lived, the Methodist societies remained in name, if not in fact, a part of the Anglican church. Separation, however, was inevitable and occurred at the death of Wesley in 1791. The newly constituted Methodist church retained some Anglican traditions such as episcopal church government and kneeling at the altar rail to receive communion. While the Anglican church lost in numbers from the separation of the Methodists, it gained in spiritual life from the movement. Many who were not members of Methodist societies were nevertheless touched by Wesley's preaching. Under John's stimulus, Anglican organizations developed to promote spiritual life and missions. The Evangelical party in the Church of England, active to this day, received strong impetus from Wesleyanism. This group also developed some of the hymns we use such as "Amazing Grace," by John Newton, the converted slave-dealing shipmaster.

Other denominations, both in England and America, felt the breath of revival which the Wesleys spread.

Continental Renewal Movements

Pietism and Moravianism fostered the new life of church renewal in Germany. Following the Thirty Years War, the state of the church had been at a low ebb. Externalism and a "dead" orthodoxy characterized many segments of the Lutheran community.

Drawing from late medieval mysticism, from Luther, and from English Puritanism, the German Pietists breathed new vigor and warmth into the church.

Philip Spener, 1635-1705, was the "Father of German Pietism." In his parish in Strasbourg, he began to gather small groups of people together for Bible study and prayer, calling these groups "associations of piety." (Eventually the term "pietism," derived from these groups, came to be used to refer to the entire movement.) Spener preached against the abuses of the day, advocated an upright life, and particularly insisted upon the experience of Christianity, not just a knowledge of it. His practices and ideas spread to other parts of Germany.

August Francke, 1663-1727, became the leading organizer of Pietism. Francke, a University professor, was touched by the pietist message. With Spener's help, Francke got an appointment as a professor at the new University of Halle, opened in 1694. At Halle, Francke, not only taught numerous students theology and the Christian life, but also organized a Bible circulating society, school for orphans, hospital, and homes for the poor. Halle became an object lesson for the Christian world.

The influence of Pietism spread informally, not through any specific new denomination. Throughout Germany and Scandinavia, Lutheran churches were touched. As with the Wesleyan movement, singing characterized Pietism. The great J. S. Bach was the organist in a Pietist-pastored church. Much of his music centered on Christian themes.

Missionary work was stimulated. Little had been done thus far by Protestants to fulfill the Great Commission. The King of Denmark, Frederick IV, sent two Halle students,

Ziegenbalg and Plutschau, to India as missionaries in 1705. The Danish king, with pietistic assistance, thus created one of the first organized missionary efforts of the modern church.

The Pietist movement has been criticized as overly legalistic, divisive, and non-intellectual. Some of the criticisms may have merit. It would appear, however, that the balance of positive contribution made by the Pietists outweighs the negatives in the process of building God's church.

Moravianism is a second example of continental renewal. Count Nicholas Zinzendorf, 1700-1760, was a devout pietistic nobleman. Although his career was public service, Christian work always captured much of his time and interest.

In 1722, a group of persecuted folk from Moravia (now Czechoslovakia) appeared in Germany seeking refuge on Zinzendorf's estate. They were a remnant of the Hussite Brethren, of pre-reformation origins. Zinzendorf allowed them to settle and eventually assumed leadership of the group. They built a settlement called Herrnhut, or House of the Lord. A powerful communion service in 1727 is often regarded as the time at which the Moravian church was actually born.

For some time it was not clear whether this group was a part of the state church of Saxony where they lived, or a separate entity. Gradually, Moravian organization grew. Eventually the church was recognized as a separate group by the government officials and spread through the German provinces.

Foreign missions became the heartthrob of the Moravians. After he had met residents of the West Indies and Greenland, Zinzendorf encouraged ministries to these areas. Dober, a potter, and Nitschmann, a carpenter, were sent to the West Indies in 1732. This approach became typical of the missionary methodology of the Moravians. They sent men who worked at a trade to support themselves, while living with and ministering to the people. They practiced "tent-making" missionary strategy, both proclaiming and living Christ. Hard places of earth were reached—Dutch Guiana, Labrador, Greenland, South Africa, and the Tibetan border. From basically a small church, over 200 missionaries were sent in about thirty years.

Zinzendorf and other Moravian leaders also ministered in America. They attempted to reach the Indians for Christ and to organize German immigrants. Moravian centers, Bethlehem, Pennsylvania and Winston-Salem, North Carolina, developed from these early years. England also witnessed Moravian expansion.

In an age when very few churches were doing anything to reach remote parts of the world for Christ, the Moravians stand out as pioneers. In spite of weaknesses, their movement provides a strong example of the building of God's church the world around.

The Results of Revival

Wesleyanism, Pietism, and Moravianism produced lasting results. Persons won to Christ and to the experience of eternal life in Him are the obvious product of these movements. In addition they encouraged other denominations to greater Christlikeness.

Less obvious, perhaps, is the impact these renewal movements had upon society. If men and women are truly Christ's, their lives make a difference in the communities in which they live. The Wesleyan movement reached the English lower classes, encouraging their upbuilding. Some writers have contended that the Wesleyan revival saved England from a revolution such as France experienced. Men whose hearts were touched by the Savior, looking about them and seeing great need, worked to improve life for others. John Howard labored to overcome the filth and squalor of English prisons. Lord Shaftesbury crusaded against cruel child labor. William Wilberforce and others attacked the slave trade and the practice of slavery from the stance of Christian compassion.

The promotion of Christian learning was enhanced by the Wesleyan revival. The British and Foreign Bible Society was founded to distribute Bibles. The Sunday school had its origins in 1780 with Anglican layman Robert Raikes. The original purpose of the Sunday school was to teach poor children, who were employed six days a week, to read and write. As other educational structures became available for that purpose, the Sunday school became the bulwark of Christian education.

Missionary work was greatly stimulated as we have noted. Although the Roman Catholics had been active since the 1500s, Protestants had been slow to spread the Gospel to the ends of the earth. In some cases, concentration on the establishment and survival of the church made it difficult to engage in foreign missionary work. In this era, Protestants came alive! The Dutch sent witnesses to what is now Indonesia. The Pietistic Danish-Halle mission served in India. The Moravians sent missionaries to many parts of the globe.

A shoemaker, William Carey, awakened England to the Great Commission. Finally, convincing other Christians of the rightness of his cause, Carey went to India where he served with distinction. Although he was not the first Protestant missionary, he is often termed the "Father of Modern Missions." His example greatly encouraged other

Englishmen to follow. Carey helped open the door, through which many others were to pass, in spreading the Gospel to the ends of the earth.

Although it faced problems in the years from 1650 to 1800, the church of Jesus Christ experienced exciting and vigorous development. Revival stimulated the building of God's church.

10

Building in a New Land

Time line   1500   1600   1700   1800   1900

While the church in Europe was building during the seventeenth and eighteenth centuries, thousands of miles to the west, the church was being planted in the New World.

Colonial Religious Groups

Religion was the motive which brought some settlers to the New World. The persecution of the Puritans in England, as we saw in chapter eight, drove them to North America. But we must not overdo the importance of religious motivation. Secular concerns—the chance to get a new start, opportunities to make more money, political oppression—probably accounted for far more immigration than religious issues.

American Christians have tended to view the colonial period through rose-colored glasses. We have looked upon the colonists as uniformly devout, pious Christians, desiring only to please God in this wilderness land and establish a new nation based upon the highest Christian ideals. We ought to know better! People then were little different from today, or from the first century for that matter. Then, as now, the proportion of real Christians was a minority of the population. They did not always reach their goals in society and politics. People operated from personal and selfish ambition.

The first persons to bring Christendom to the New World were Roman Catholics. Spanish and Portuguese explorers and conquerors brought Franciscan, Dominican, and Jesuit monks with them. Churches were established for Spanish immigrants and Indian converts. Universities were founded, considerably earlier than the first English settlements. St. Augustine, Florida, the first permanent white settlement in what is now the United States, was Spanish and Roman Catholic. In what is now New Mexico, over 15,000 Indian converts had been made to Catholicism by 1621, just one year after the Mayflower. The French also sent priests to their Canadian, Great Lakes, and Mississippi valley holdings in the early 1600s.

But it was the English who most influenced the development of North America and laid foundations for the building of God's church in the New World. Religious practice in the English Atlantic seaboard colonies varied widely.

The Anglicans, not surprisingly, were the first English group in America. From the earliest days of the Jamestown colony in Virginia, founded in 1607, Robert Hunt, a company chaplain, served the Lord's Supper to colonists seated on logs under the cover of an old sail. The rudiments of a parish system were begun by 1620. Although it was difficult to obtain ministers from far-away England, the Anglican church grew and became the established state church in Virginia in 1625. Anglicans held leading positions in several of the colonies and their church became the state church throughout the south. An English organization, the Society for the Propagation of the Gospel in Foreign Parts, sent over 300 missionaries to plant churches. By 1776, a total of 480 churches had been founded by Anglicans.

Congregationalists were the most important church group in the northern colonies. A few, such as the glamorized "Pilgrim" settlers in Plymouth, were separatists in England, desiring complete separation of church from state. Most, however, were Puritan independents who desired congregational authority within a state church. Centering in Boston, these independents came to dominate New England. Congregationalism became the established state church in the New England colonies. Schools were established, including Harvard University, for the training of pastors. A Calvinistic theology was vigorously taught. A strict life style prevailed. Singing of psalms was a joyous and significant part of worship. By 1776, there were 658 Congregational meeting houses in the colonies.

Ousted from Massachusetts by Congregationalist leaders, Roger Williams became an important figure in Baptist beginnings in the New World. Williams received permission from London to establish Rhode Island colony for the "distressed of conscience." In Providence and Newport, churches of baptistic persuasion were begun in the late 1630s and early 1640s. Other Baptist groups sprang up in the other colonies and often faced strong persecution. After fifty years, only about fifty very small Baptist churches existed. Events of the 1700s, however, changed that. By 1776, there were 497.

King Charles II granted a charter to William Penn for a colony which became the center of Quaker religious life in America. Some Quakers had come to the New World previously. Pennsylvania, which offered the Quakers not only toleration but active government favor, became their leading center. Penn himself worked diligently for the Quaker cause. In the later colonial era, the Quakers declined somewhat in vigor from their earlier aggressive days. They had 298 churches in 1776.

A similar charter grant was made to Roman Catholic George Calvert, Lord Baltimore, for Maryland colony as a haven for his co-religionists. Few Catholics came, so the colony was opened to all. Roman Catholics in Maryland became strong advocates of religious toleration and freedom. The Baltimore area was the principal center of Catholic organization in early America. Catholicism was comparatively weak in colonial America. By 1776 only fifty churches existed. The great immigration of the nineteenth century was to change that.

The Dutch commercial venture in New Amsterdam ("New York" when the English took it over) introduced the Dutch Reformed faith to America. The Collegiate Reformed Church in New York City is a modern descendant of these early beginnings. By 1776, the Dutch Reformed had established 123 churches, most of them in the New York-New Jersey area.

German immigrants came in considerable numbers, especially to Pennsylvania. Many were irreligious, but others established churches. Henry Muhlenberg led the scattered Lutherans in the organization of churches and a synod. By 1776, they had 151 congregations. German Reformed groups were established as well. Mennonites arrived as early as 1683 at Germantown, and Philadelphia. Lancaster County became their principle center.

Presbyterianism in America is the result of a blend of English Puritan Congregationalism, which adopted Presbyterian church government, and Scotch-Irish immigration. In 1692 the First Presbyterian Church of Philadelphia was started in a warehouse. It was the first

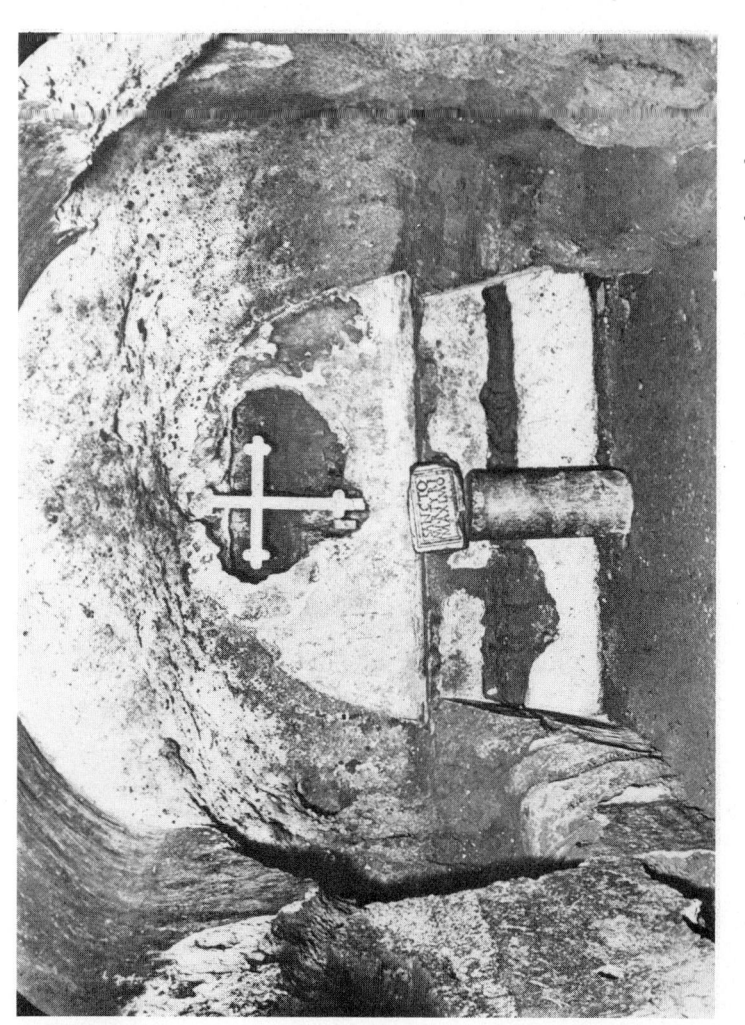

Ancient Church in Rome

Augustine Preaching

Luther Burning the Papal Bull

Luther's Trial in Worms

church to bear that name in America. The upland areas of Pennsylvania and the south became centers of Scotch-Irish Presbyterianism. Francis Makemie, who organized the Philadelphia Presbytery in 1706, has often been termed the "Father of American Presbyterianism" for his effective leadership. Presbyterians grew remarkably in the 1700s. As a result they had 453 churches by 1776.

Religious practice centered on Sunday in the colonies. The meeting house was the center of activity. The first buildings were crude. By the Revolution, some gorgeous churches were in use. Seats were often assigned to families. Churches were unheated, so foot stoves and fur bags were used for warmth. Sermons were long. A Dutch traveler recorded a four-hour prayer in a New England church!

Religious abuses from Europe sometimes crossed the Atlantic. The witch scare which swept England in the 1640s reached America. In Salem, Massachusetts twenty were executed for witchcraft.

The Protestant groups of colonial America all placed stress upon the Bible in worship and preaching. It is likely that elements of the body of Christ, the true church, existed among them all. But they tended to be shortsighted with regard to reaching the Indian population. Some—John Elliot, David Brainerd, the Moravians—expended effort in this direction. For the most part, however, colonial Americans were indifferent, if not hostile, to their Indian neighbors.

The Great Awakening

In spite of the number of groups in America, religion in the colonies was still for the few. Church membership was not automatic, as it had been in Europe. Poverty made difficult the hiring of a pastor and the building of church buildings. Illiteracy hindered Bible study. Great distances, in the south especially, made it hard to gather congregations. Preoccupation with economic progress crowded out spiritual concern.

Some Christians became concerned about the secularism of colonial society. Dutch Reformed pastor Theodore Freylinghuysen, for example, began to travel about New Jersey preaching the message of salvation. Presbyterians William and Gilbert Tennent did similar work. Great excitement followed. English evangelist George Whitefield came in 1739 and broadened the scope of the burgeoning revival. The Rhode Island legislature even adjourned its sessions to listen to Whitefield preach!

In New England, pastor Jonathan Edwards was a key figure. Edwards was one of the outstanding men of colonial America. Not only was he a devout pastor, he also was a thorough student and gifted writer. Edwards preached widely in the New England colonies. Although he was a manuscript preacher, his sermons, like the famous "Sinners in the Hands of an Angry God," made a great impact.

In the south, the Great Awakening bore the mark of the frontier as revival made its image especially in the upland districts. Cutting across denominational lines, the revival strengthened Baptist and Presbyterian churches greatly, but touched other groups as well. Both Baptists and Presbyterians founded many new churches and organized new associations and presbyteries. The Anglican clergy and leadership of the coast opposed these developments, particularly the emotional extremes which sometimes accompanied the Great Awakening. One Baptist pastor was thrown into a frontier stockade jail but continued to preach from the inside as his congregation gathered about the outside!

The Great Awakening made an important impact. Many

were won to Christ in the period from the 1720s to the 1760s. New churches were founded. Schools were established, including those which were the forerunners of Princeton, Dartmouth, and Pennsylvania universities.

But along with the benefits came problems and division. Some churchmen felt revival was an unworthy method of church development. Several denominations were split as a result. Congregationalists in New England contended bitterly with one another. Baptists divided. Perhaps most significantly, the Presbyterians broke apart into "New Side" and "Old Side" factions.

The tone of American Protestantism, however, for one hundred years to come, was set by the Great Awakening. Evangelical emphases would be at the forefront. Preaching would be fervent and personal. Experiential Christianity, rather than liturgical or sacramental religion, would hold a dominant place.

It has been contended that the Great Awakening encouraged the development of democratic principles and practice. Those whose religious beliefs demanded it, urged the elimination of the established Anglican church in Virginia and Congregational church in New England. These experiences may have contributed to similar demands for more democratic patterns in political matters as well.

The Revolutionary Period

The revival movement ended with the onset of the Revolutionary War. One might think that the dangers of war would contribute to spiritual hunger. Studies prove just the opposite. Political grievances, defeating the British, and building a new nation preoccupied Americans for the next generation.

Americans were divided about the war. The most vigorous advocates of the Patriot cause were the Congregationalists. The Presbyterians, German groups, and Baptists also generally favored independence. The Anglicans were divided. Several leading patriots had Anglican backgrounds. But most of the Americans who were Tories, that is, those favored maintaining unity with Great Britain, were Anglicans. Mennonites and Quakers were neutral, opposing warfare on principle. Pulpits rang with pronouncements favoring one side or the other.

With the signing of peace, the churches set up constitutions and organizations of a national nature. The Anglicans suffered through the loss of many Tories who had left for Canada. The very name "Church of England" was unpopular. Eventually a new name, Protestant Episcopal, was adopted, and a distinct American organization, with its own bishop, William White, was instituted. Methodism had begun to touch America, but its parent organization in Britain was still Anglican. John Wesley himself, in 1784, appointed Francis Asbury and Thomas Coke to reorganize emerging American Methodism as a separate entity.

Other churches found reorganization easier. Dutch and German Reformed churches were already largely independent of Europe. Roman Catholics maintained their ties with Rome but loosened ties with English Catholics. The first American Catholic bishop, John Carroll, was consecrated in 1790 as the bishop of Baltimore. Congregationalists, Baptists, Presbyterians, and Lutherans were already independent but sharpened their national organizational focus. Quakers were hindered somewhat by the war in that their pacifism caused them to turn more inward. Some segments of that church, especially in the east, tended to become more hereditary and quietistic than they had been before.

The Revolution era produced new liberal elements in American religion. In 1785, King's Chapel openly affiliated with the Unitarian position. Other churches followed. New England Congregationalism was hit hard by these defections. Harvard University was won by Unitarian leadership.

The Universalist church was also founded in the revolutionary period by John Murray. This group believed that ultimately all people would be saved. The Unitarians and Universalists were somewhat similar and have united into one denomination in recent times.

Probably the most significant religious development of the Revolutionary War era was the enactment of the religious liberty statements in the federal Constitution. Article VI indicates that no religious test shall be required for public office. Bill of Rights Amendment I states that Congress shall make no laws establishing religion or prohibiting its free exercise.

The various states were slow to drop their legal establishments. Massachusetts was the last to do so, rescinding Congregational established status in 1833. The federal government, however, did not at any time establish one church as a national state church.

The reasons behind this significant provision are many. The religious groups in the new nation were many and varied. Which one would be selected if a state church were decided upon? Old World persecution suggested religious liberty as a wise policy. Economic advancement would be enhanced if all persons could be included in production, labor, and market considerations. The liberal thinkers of an Enlightenment, deistic bent, like Franklin and Jefferson, urged a religious liberty policy. But so did some Christians. Baptists, especially, urgently petitioned the Continental

Convention advocating religious liberty. Their longstanding heritage demanded this position.

The principle of voluntarism, which was now the basis of American religion, was to prove of great benefit to the Gospel. The church would have to develop according to the personal commitment of its membership, not because of government sponsorship or promotion. This called forth sacrifice, service, and hard work from American Christians. By the same token, governmental direction of church life has been minimal, allowing freedom for expression, outreach, and experimentation.

Denominationalism as a feature of religious life was really born in America. In Europe the concept of an established church with opposing sects or dissenting groups had evolved. Here the idea of several, more or less equal, competing groups across a wide religious spectrum came to be accepted as the norm. This arrangement was to produce great diversity and sometimes great division, but it was also to bring about great vitality and health.

The setting was rugged and new. Christians brought to America their religious practices and labels from the Old World. But here, they evolved into distinctively American forms. God was building His church in a new land. It was to become a church of impressive strength.

11

Building on the Frontier

Time line   1600   1700   1800   1900   2000

America was expanding dramatically in the early years of the nineteenth century. Across the Allegheny Mountains poured thousands of settlers, eager for the new land of the Mississippi Valley. The church of Jesus Christ had declined in growth and vitality in the closing decades of the eighteenth century. The settlers of the west often were ill-educated and irreligious. Greed for land and moral carelessness were prevalent. It was imperative that these unfavorable trends be reversed if America was to be reached with the Gospel.

The Second Great Awakening

The visitation of God, which has often been called the Second Great Awakening, began at Yale College in the late 1790s. Yale had been founded by devout Congregationalists as a Christian institution when Harvard defected to Unitarianism. But Yale, reflecting society at large, had only one professing Christian in its entering class of 1796. The President, Dr. Timothy Dwight, engaged in a series of debates on vital Christian issues. The stance of deism and intellectual pride faded as conviction and conversion swept the campus.

From Yale, revival spread to Williams College and throughout New England. Men who were to become leaders of the church for years to come were converted through the Yale revival. As they pastored churches, they carried a zeal for God with them.

West of the mountains, the Second Great Awakening was to make an even more dynamic impact than on the Atlantic seaboard. Several methods were utilized to proclaim the Gospel. Circuit riding preachers traveled across the countryside with the good news. They wore the simplest of clothing, forded swollen streams, talked to isolated people in lonely cabins, and sold Christian books. The Methodists, particularly, rode the circuit with great effect. Since the circuit rider received little salary, he lived from the gifts of those to whom he ministered. Few could support a family, so most circuit riders were very young, in their late teens or early twenties.

The farmer-preacher was the dominant figure of Baptist ministry on the frontier. A local layman would be selected to be the pastor of the small congregation. Farming all week and preaching on Sunday, he understood thoroughly the toils and heartaches of his congregation.

The frontier camp meeting was another method of evangelism in the church of the new west. In August of 1801, near Cane Ridge, Kentucky, the most extravagant and famous of all camp meetings was held. As many as 20,000 people gathered from many states to sing, hear preaching from several preaching points, and respond to the Christian message. Presbyterian Barton Stone was the leader of this great gathering.

Cane Ridge became the model for other camp meetings which sprang up all across the frontier. Presbyterians and Baptists also convened gatherings, but it was the

Methodists who most frequently and effectively utilized them. They became Methodism's "harvest time."

The camp meeting physical set-up consisted of a central clearing, where half-log benches were placed. An elevated preaching stand and an area for seekers to pray were built at the front. Surrounding the meeting area were the tents and wagons of those attending. Such modern facilities as dining halls, comfortable chapels, and recreational facilities were unknown.

The people came from all walks of life. Some were devout Christians; others had no interest in the Gospel but came because this was the single exciting social event in the area. As the message of the Gospel touched them, people responded emotionally. Some fainted, some jerked their heads and limbs from side to side, others danced and barked like dogs. To control these emotional excesses and bring people to a lucid conversion experience was the great concern of camp leaders.

Both in camp meetings and in the regular meetings of the church, preaching, then as now, was a vital method of evangelism and edification. In the west, an extemporaneous style developed in the pulpit. The eastern method of manuscript reading was shunned as unspiritual. Loud, bombastic deliveries with a quavering "preacher's tone" were the style of the day.

Some of the preachers of that era were of heroic mold. Peter Cartwright, Methodist circuit rider, for example, traveled miles to share the Gospel with remote settlers. Bold and fearless, Cartwright tackled either intellectually or physically those who opposed Christianity. A man among men, he related well with the rugged frontier life of the Ohio Valley where he lived and served. In 1846 he lost a race for the United States Congress to the rail-splitter who later became famous, Abraham Lincoln.

Other preachers were characterized by eccentricity. Lorenzo Dow built a reputation as "Crazy Dow," a name which was sure to add to his crowd as he visited a community. With long, untrimmed hair and beard, Dow did the unexpected as he preached: having a lad blow a trumpet at a dramatic moment from a high tree as he spoke on the Second Coming, smashing furniture, and seeming near death as he spoke.

Singing was another important method of church life in this era. The hymns of Wesley and Watts, popular on the east coast, were supplemented by new, lively folk music with a Christian message. Sung a cappella and accompanied by swaying and clapping, these songs fit the culture of the west. The church, throughout much of its history, has expressed its message in music forms which were indigenous to its culture. This approach has continued in our day in the Gospel song and in contemporary forms of musical expression.

As the new districts west of the Alleghenies became more settled, rural methods were modified and town evangelistic campaigns were begun. They were termed "protracted meetings" since they were held over days or weeks of time.

Charles G. Finney, the converted lawyer, was the evangelist best known for this form. Presbyterian Finney held his meetings in churches or halls and urged convicted sinners to come forward to "anxious seats" near the front. The camp meeting's "altar" for prayer and Finney's "anxious seat" were the origin of the practice of coming forward to an altar to seek God, as used in our century. Finney's campaigns in upstate New York, Ohio, and elsewhere brought many people to Christ. He also became a principal defender of revival and a promoter of its techniques.

In 1857 and 1858 another renewal and evangelism

movement warmed the church. In New York and Philadelphia, laymen gathered early in the mornings and at noon for times of prayer and discussion. Generally without significant preaching, this lay movement was also responsible for leading many to Christ.

The results of the Second Great Awakening were broad and deep. Many were converted to Christ. Churches were born, developed, and thrived. Church membership statistics increased. (In that day, membership was a significant measuring device in that most Protestant churches demanded a conversion account to belong.) Church life blossomed. The practice of midweek times for congregational prayer was born here.

Broader international and social issues were affected. A group of students at Williams College, later known as the Haystack group because they met under a haystack during a storm, became concerned for foreign missions. The result was the first American missionary organization, the American Board of Commissioners for Foreign Missions (Congregational). The Board sent its first missionaries— Adoniram Judson and Luther Rice—to the field in 1812. When Judson and Rice became Baptists en route to India and Burma, the Congregationalists found others to replace them. But the Baptists had to organize a society to support missionaries already on the field! The result was to expand missionary outreach in both groups. Presbyterians, Methodists, and others followed until America became a primary sending base for missionaries.

Educational work was stimulated by revival as well. The American Bible Society (1816) and the American Sunday School Union, now the American Missionary Fellowship (1817) are two of the organizations from this era of revival.

Societies were formed to oppose evils of the day: the liquor trade, war, the abuse of women, unjust prison conditions, mistreatment of the mentally ill and the poor, and slavery. Social reform was not the essence of religion to nineteenth century American Christians as it has become to some in the twentieth century. Neither, however, was it something irrelevant and unworthy of a Christian. Concern for the suffering was an outgrowth of a spiritually quickened heart and conscience. Nineteenth century evangelicals were at the forefront of social reform movements.

Denominational Developments

The Anglicans (Episcopalians) and Congregationalists had been the largest and most influential denominations in colonial America. During the early nineteenth century, they were replaced by the Baptists and Methodists, who have remained as the largest Protestant churches in the nation. These two groups seemingly best adapted to the new frontier nature of America. It was an age of firm belief in democracy. The Baptists with their democratic church government and the Methodists with their democratic Arminian theology fit the image well.

The Episcopalians, with their formal worship patterns, did not win wide acceptance on the frontier. As a result, their influence declined. The Quakers, also prominent in colonial America, were quietistic in their religious approach so they, too, had limited response in the new and bombastic west.

Congregationalism faced a different kind of problem. The liberal trend in New England churches, developed in the Revolutionary era, increased. Small groups, segments of congregations, and whole churches openly became Unitarian. William Channing, pastor of the Federal Street Church in Boston, emerged as the spokesman of the

Unitarians. In 1825 the American Unitarian Association of 125 congregations was formed, most of them in New England. Orthodox Congregationalists, led by clergyman Lyman Beecher, endeavored to stem the tide by biblical preaching and evangelistic work.

Presbyterianism expanded into the west in these years. Finney and his followers encouraged an aggressive evangelism and introduced a semi-Arminian theology. Both forces affected the Presbyterian church. The strong Calvinists, who opposed Finney's doctrines and practices, separated, in 1837, from the Finneyite New School Presbyterians, producing two organizations. The German Reformed Church also suffered division over revival issues.

Thomas Campbell, Pennsylvania pastor, weary of the denominational wrangling and strife typical of the period, formed a group of people who protested against this hyper-sectarianism. They wanted to be simply "Christians." By 1850 the group had grown widely and eventually became the Disciples of Christ or Christian Church. Stressing the New Testament church as a pattern and baptism as a part of salvation, Campbell's descendants have since taken the labels Disciples of Christ, Christian Church, or Church of Christ.

The early years of the nineteenth century witnessed great growth of Lutheranism in America. Waves of German and Scandinavian immigrants came to the upper midwestern states, there to develop many synodical organizations according to ethnic derivation and theological and church-practice distinctives. One of the most influential of these groups was the Missouri Synod, founded by conservative, German Lutherans in 1847, led by Carl Walther.

Roman Catholicism was strengthened tremendously by

the immigrant influx. The Irish were the earliest ethnic Catholic group to reach America in large numbers. Almost one million Irish had come to the United States by 1850, most of them Catholic. The large cities of the northeast were to be their new homes and the Roman Catholic Church the focal point of their lives. Next came the German Catholic immigrants, who settled in the farms and towns of the midwest. Conflicts developed at times between the Irish and Germans over church leadership and policy.

The Catholic church assisted the immigrant in securing housing, employment, and understanding of American ways. Parochial schools were established, often as a protest against the Protestant tone of available education. Georgetown College was founded as were charitable institutions and publication organizations. By the Civil War, Roman Catholicism was one of the largest of American religious groups, exerting a strong influence in urban areas.

In Canada in the early nineteenth century, Roman Catholicism was the prevailing faith in French Quebec and among the many Irish immigrants to British North America. The strongest Protestant groups were the Church of England and the Presbyterians, although Methodists, Baptists, and Congregationalists had representation.

Cults and Extremists

Democracy and the principle of voluntarism in religion produced a climate of freedom conducive to the rapid growth of the church. But that same climate of individualism made possible the proliferation of extremist groups, cults, and non-Christian organizations. The tendency toward emotional excess and suspicion of intellectualism contributed to this trend.

In the 1840s and 1850s a keen interest in the doctrine of the Second Coming of Christ emerged among many Christians. An unlearned farmer, William Miller, became the leading voice in this movement. Tragically, Miller added his own concepts to biblical revelation. He arrived at the dates 1843 and then a revision to 1844 for Christ's return. Great excitement prevailed, meetings were held, huge charts were drawn. With the failure of his predictions, bitterness and disillusionment prevailed. His followers drifted into other groups—the Advent Christian Church, the Seventh-Day Adventist Church, and the Shakers.

The teen-age Fox sisters in Rochester, New York, in the 1840s, as a prank produced some unusual noises and sights. Taking advantage of the high interest in the occult of the period, an older sister began to hold public seances featuring the girls. Soon an organization of their followers was formed which became the Spiritualist movement.

Mormonism was the largest of the early nineteenth century cultic groups. Joseph Smith, supposedly receiving revelation through some mysterious golden plates, provided the *Book of Mormon* as a revelation for a new belief. Gathering followers from widespread areas, Smith moved his group from New York to Ohio, Missouri, and then Illinois, where he was jailed and murdered in 1844. Shortly thereafter, Brigham Young led the main body of the Church of Latter Day Saints to its new home in Utah, where it has flourished since. A smaller segment, the Reorganized Church of the Latter Day Saints, remained headquartered in the midwest.

Communal groups existed briefly on the frontier. The Shakers were among the communalists. Followers of Anne Lee, the supposed feminine manifestation of Christ in a return to earth, the Shakers set up nineteen communal farms where they lived strict, regimented lives. Their worship was characterized by shaking and ritual dancing. Since they were strictly celibate, the group declined in numbers and died.

The Oneida Community was another communal, extremist group. These people, followers of John Noyes, believed in a perfectionism which said that everything the elect did was free from sin. All things were to be shared, including wives and husbands. The Oneida cultists went into the silver business, dropped their extreme beliefs, and eventually abandoned all religious aspects.

The Germans, with their tradition of strong discipline, obedience, and hard work, made good communalists. The Zoar community, the Rappites, and the Amana colony are examples of German, semi-religious communes.

Extremism surfaced in the religious community in other ways. Protestants went beyond mere opposition to Roman Catholic doctrine to vigorous opposition to Catholic people, even to open persecution at times. Catholics were not above returning the hatred. Anti-immigrant political and social movements were tinged with religious overtones.

Denominations fought each other with the invective of a political campaign. A society which was often suspicious of research and cautious evaluation tended to favor simplistic solutions to problems.

The Civil War Era

The issue of slavery disrupted the church in the decades prior to the outbreak of the Civil War. Finney's convert, Theodore Weld, was an outspoken champion of Christian anti-slavery sentiment. Southern preachers defended the practice. As a result, schisms tore many denominations apart.

The Methodists lost a segment of their numbers in 1843

with the departure of the Wesleyan Methodist movement (the Wesleyan church today). The major schism, however, took place in 1845 when the church divided north and south over the issue of a slave-holding bishop. The two segments were not reunited until 1939.

Baptists also divided in 1845 over the issue of the appointment of a slave-holding missionary. The Southern Baptist Convention was founded in that year. The northern Baptists organized in associations until 1907 when the Northern Baptist Convention (now American Baptist) was formed. The two groups remain separate to this day.

Presbyterians had previously divided into Old School and New School groups over the practice of revival. Both of these segments further divided over slavery, so for a time there were four major Presbyterian bodies. After the Civil War, the two northern groups and the two southern groups reunited to form the bases of the present two major Presbyterian churches in America today.

Both sides invoked the aid of Divine Providence during the war. Both held prayer meetings and revival services. It was a military struggle with strong religious overtones.

After the conflict, the development of Black churches wrought a major change in the religious picture. Prior to emancipation, Blacks tended to worship in the churches of their white masters. Now they were free to develop their own organizations. Baptist and Methodist churches were formed among them in great numbers. Eventually the National Baptist Convention, organized in 1866, and the African Methodist Episcopal Church were established on the national level. The church provided the vehicle of cultural and religious expression for the freedman. It also gave opportunity for leadership which few other organizations provided.

In spite of cults and extremists, division and war, the

early nineteenth century was a period of exciting growth and development in the church of Jesus Christ. The "gung-ho" all-or-nothing approach of the day became most appealing when directed by biblical teaching to the person of Christ. God's church was being built in great strength across the new frontiers of a new land.

12

Building in the Modern Age

Time line   1700   1800   1900   2000

Although complexities and problems surfaced to provide major challenges, the church of God continued to build vigorously in North America in the late 1800s and 1900s.

New Americans

After Appomattox, the rate of immigration into the United States increased tremendously. Lutheran bodies in the upper midwest were strengthened by the newcomers. So was the Roman Catholic Church. The Civil War had not divided the Catholic church significantly, nor was that body active in ministering to the newly freed Black. Catholicism's energy and money were spent ministering to the immigrant population. The latter part of the nineteenth century brought a shift in immigration patterns. Earlier, northern and western Europe had sent most of the newcomers; now they came from southern and eastern Europe. Polish and Italian enclaves in large cities were the new focus of Catholic work.

The struggle to serve the immigrants brought Catholicism to one of its major crises. Catholic leaders like Archbishops Ireland of St. Paul and Gibbons of Baltimore felt that Catholicism should enter the mainstream of American life as quickly as possible. Others, the Germans especially, felt that this trend was destroying the essential fabric of Catholicism. Actual accusations of heresy were leveled against these "Americanizers," demonstrating the depth of ethnic division within the church. Ethnic parishes still exert a strong influence in many parts of American Catholicism.

By the early twentieth century, the Roman Catholic Church had come of age in America. In 1908, the American church received status equal to other branches of the church; no longer was it regarded as a missionary nation. World War I brought Catholics into wider social contact with other Americans, bringing public acceptance. The work of Father John Ryan in social welfare and the television ministry of Bishop Fulton Sheen increased understanding. The election of John Kennedy to the Presidency in 1960 seems to have marked the full recognition of Roman Catholics in American life.

Other religious traditions also were strengthened by immigration. The evangelical Protestant stance, which had dominated early nineteenth century America, was being replaced by an increasing pluralism in religious life. A wave of Jewish immigrants poured into the United States in the decades following 1880, caused by persecution in eastern Europe. Some of these immigrants were anti-religious, but others among them associated with the Orthodox, Conservative, or Reform synagogues of northeastern cities where they settled.

Other newcomers from eastern Europe were of Orthodox religious persuasion. They established Russian, Greek, Serbian, Rumanian, or Bulgarian Orthodox churches in the urban centers to which they came.

Tensions continued between the older citizens and

immigrant settlers. Catholics attacked public schools, and Protestants criticized Catholic undemocratic methods, intemperance, and lack of Sabbath observance. *The Menace*, a leading nativist publication, urged readers to "Read *The Menace*, get the dope; go to the polls, defeat the pope." Nativism conflicts existed strongly until the First World War.

Challenges to the Church

Liberal theological beliefs have provided a major challenge to the building of the church over the last century. Darwinian evolution, German textual criticism, and modern sociology and psychology have produced an intellectual threat which cannot be ignored. The Presbyterian church was rocked by the heresy trials of Charles Biggs and Preserved Smith. Robert Ingersoll ranged across America lecturing against Christianity. Northern Baptists, Methodists, and Congregationalists were infected strongly with liberal theological views. The authority of the Bible was the central issue to the debate.

Conservatives responded with statements of defense of the faith. Benjamin B. Warfield, J. G. Machen, and A. H. Strong provided theological support for the conservative position. The Niagara Bible Conference of 1895 issued a statement defining five "fundamentals," or key doctrines of Christian orthodoxy: inerrancy of the Bible, deity and virgin birth of Christ, substitutionary atonement, resurrection of Christ, and His bodily return to earth. Those who accepted the dispensationalist view of theology following John Nelson Darby from England, as well as others, came to champion the "fundamentalist" cause. Three million copies of a 12-volume, paperback set, *The*

Fundamentals, were sent to religious leaders. The project was funded by laymen Milton and Lyman Stewart.

The 1920s saw the climax of this fundamentalist vs. modernist conflict. Literary and academic voices led the nation in a spirit of opposition to religious values and restraint in general. Harry Emerson Fosdick was perhaps the most able advocate of liberal thought. The famed Scopes trial in 1925, with liberal Clarence Darrow pitted against politician and conservative William Jennings Bryan, brought wide media attention to the debate. Liberal leadership was able to capture control of many of the major denominations. For twenty years, the conservative cause was to be isolated, divided, and muted. Theological liberalism assumed the primary position in American Protestantism, until it was modified by neo-orthodoxy in the 1950s.

Another challenge to the church was the unreached masses in newly urban America. Mission work was begun among skid row inhabitants of the great cities. Churches attempted to reach newly arrived immigrants. The needs of urban workers called forth the so-called social gospel movement which attempted to bring Christian concern to bear upon the social problems of the late nineteenth century. In some instances, but not all, social reform movements in this era were based upon liberal theological positions. Conservatives, too, demonstrated concern for the needs of the urban masses.

Cults continued to flourish. Theosophy, founded by Helena Blavatsky, combined Buddhism and Spiritualism to gather followers. Christian Science, established by Mary Baker Eddy, promoted mental health. Unity, led by Charles and Myrtle Fillmore, stressed the power of positive thinking. The Jehovah's Witnesses were the most successful of the newer American cults. Founded by

Charles Russell, but built by Joseph (Judge) Rutherford the Kingdom Halls and *Watchtower* publications of this group multiplied across the land.

Other challenges to Christianity came from the secular culture surrounding the church. The twentieth century brought the horrors of two world wars with resulting suffering and death. In 1914, many churchmen looked upon the conflict as a holy crusade. World War II was not so "sanctified," but its monstrous tyranny and devastating loss of life brought worldwide disillusionment and despair in its wake.

Atheistic Marxist communism has been a major challenge to the church in the past forty years. Not only have vast areas of the world been closed to Christian witness because of this governmental philosophy, but non-Christian intellectual life in the west has found strength and support from its concepts.

Although immorality has always been a challenge to the church, the past century has seen a greater acceptance of immorality. Crime, drunkenness, sexual promiscuity, government corruption, and the breakdown of the family are but a few of the moral problems the church of the twentieth century must face.

The Growth of the Church

While problems and challenges have confronted the church in the last 100 years, great opportunities for growth have also been available. After the Civil War, new areas of the Rocky Mountain and Pacific west opened for settlement. The churches established Home Missions programs to spread the Gospel into these areas. The miner, logger, and cowboy of the west were less responsive to Christianity than the settled and family-oriented farmer of the midwest. Although the west remains one of the least "churched" parts of America, some congregations were begun and the good news was received in some lives.

Throughout the nineteenth century, American Christians had enlarged their role in world missionary outreach. This international concern was heightened in the latter decades of the century when American economic and political interests expanded abroad. As secular news gave increased attention to foreign countries, Christians became more aware of the spiritual need of overseas peoples. The denominations increased their missionary concern, giving, and staffs. The Student Volunteer Movement, led by John R. Mott, had as its slogan, "The evangelization of the world in this generation." For thirty years this organization enlisted keen collegians who went to the ends of the earth for Christ.

The birth of the Christian and Missionary Alliance took place in this international climate. Albert B. Simpson, 1843-1919, Canadian-born Presbyterian, was the father of the C&MA. Simpson pastored churches in Ontario and Kentucky before assuming a prominent pulpit in New York City. Leaving the Presbyterian church to reach neglected people, Simpson founded an independent congregation in that city.

His great concerns were for the evangelization of the neglected peoples around him, the experience of a deeper Christian life in the Spirit, the ministry of physical healing, and the preaching of the Second Coming of Christ. Simpson gathered an ever-increasing number of like-minded people about him. They established a publishing house, a periodical, a Bible school, a missionary sending organization, and (although he would deny it) eventually a denomination. His intent was never to establish churches in competition with existing congregations. But when independent "tabernacles" sprang up, he was virtually forced to assist and shepherd them.

Through the years which have followed, the Christian and Missionary Alliance has grown into a fully developed denominational body. The World War II era witnessed significant numerical growth which has continued since that time. Over 1600 Alliance churches present the gospel of Christ in North America today. Local churches are organized into twenty-three districts.

Ministries are maintained by the C&MA among ethnics such as Spanish-speaking, Indian, Chinese, Black, Eskimo, mountain people, French Canadian, Vietnamese, Cambodian, and Hmong. While the Alliance has come of age denominationally, it has not forgotten its original focus: aggressive foreign missionary outreach.

The agencies of evangelism which gave birth to the Alliance and other new denominations continued to be effective tools for growth during the nineteenth century. The local church programs were enhanced by the Sunday school movement. Great conventions were held to promote the Sunday school; publishers began to produce literature and teaching aids for use in the local church.

Mass evangelism continued to be used as a means of growth. Dwight L. Moody, 1837-1899, was the leading evangelist of the later nineteenth century. He systematized revivalism in the great cities of America and Great Britain. Moody was not a theologian, but rather a businessman and Y.M.C.A. secretary. Assisted by musician Ira Sankey, Moody used a colloquial preaching style and spiritual earnestness which gained a wide hearing across denominational lines.

Billy Sunday, 1862-1935, was a professional baseball player who became a leading evangelist in early twentieth century America. Sunday was a controversial figure. His sincere preaching won many to Christ, but his coarse antics discredited his message among some sophisticated Americans.

Billy Graham, born in 1918, has been the central figure of evangelical Christians for the past thirty years. Vaulted into prominence by the Hearst press in his Los Angeles campaign in 1949, Graham has occupied the attention of increasing numbers of people. His city-wide campaigns, periodicals, books, secular appearances, and television ministry have been significant tools in the proclamation of the Gospel.

The free-wheeling 1920s, the economically troubled 1930s, and the war-oriented 1940s were not years of great evangelical strength in America. In the 1950s, something of a religious upswing could be observed. Church attendance, giving, and church building construction increased. Although this increased interest cannot always be described as thoroughly evangelical, it may well indicate the spiritual hunger of the period and dissatisfaction with materialistic goals.

The political and social upheavals which struck the United States in the 1960s may have brought that spiritual hunger to a peak. Large numbers of alienated young people, some from counter-cultural settings, were won to Christ in the so-called Jesus Movement. While it is too early to assess the strength and impact of the movement fully, churches across the nation received an infusion of new vitality through this phenomenon.

Denominational Life

Throughout the past century, new church groups have been created to give additional vehicles for the building of God's church. Disaffected Methodists who felt Wesley's doctrines of regeneration and sanctification were being neglected in their churches, left that denomination in large numbers. Some organized the Free Methodist Church in 1860. Others established the Church of God (Anderson, Indiana) in 1881. The largest Wesleyan group to be built was the Church of the Nazarene, resulting from the 1908 merger of several groups. Phineas Breeze, California pastor, was the key leader in early Nazarene development.

In 1857 a conservative wing of the Dutch Reformed Church separated to establish the Christian Reformed Church. They considered this action a "return" to essential Calvinistic principles. Rev. K. Vanden Bosch was an outstanding leader of this group.

Pentecostalism had its origins about the turn of the century. An emphasis upon speaking in tongues as the evidence of the filling of the Holy Spirit appeared among separate groups of believers—in the hill country of North Carolina and Tennessee, in Rev. Charles F. Parham's Bible School in Kansas, and in the Azuza Street Mission in Los Angeles. The Church of God (Cleveland, Tennessee) became the strongest southern Pentecostal denomination and the Assembly of God, founded in 1914, the largest in the north and west. Aimee Semple McPherson, with her flamboyant Angeles Temple in Los Angeles, founded yet another Pentecostal group, the Church of the Foursquare Gospel. American Blacks have been won in increasing numbers to the Pentecostal cause, particularly to the Church of God in Christ denomination. Pentecostalism has made a major impact through its foreign missions programs and its outreach to neglected, lower economic groups.

The appeal of speaking in tongues, spiritual sharing, and warmth of religious experience has also been emphasized by the charismatic movement. Cutting across all denominational lines, and finding great strength among Roman Catholic, Lutheran, and Episcopal churchmen, this trend appears to be a major phenomenon of the twentieth century church in America. It seems too early to assess its full impact.

New Baptist groups also have appeared in recent years. In protest over liberal trends, the General Association of Regular Baptists was organized in 1932. Another northern Baptist break took place fifteen years later in the establishment of the Conservative Baptist Association. German Baptists established their own conference, the North American Baptist Association, and Swedish Baptists formed the Baptist General Conference. These four groups, in addition to numerous others, have expanded to provide a significant evangelical voice.

Churches of Scandinavian origin—the Covenant Church founded in Sweden by Karl Rosenius, and the Evangelical Free Church, of Swedish and Norwegian background—have also developed. The establishment of Independent Fundamental Churches of America, Bible churches, and Bible Presbyterian churches represents yet another aspect of the proliferation of new church bodies.

In Canada, the vigor and growth of the church has been seen through increased outreach to others across western Canada and to foreign soil. In 1925 Methodists, Congregationalists, and most Presbyterians merged into the United Church of Canada. Along with the Church of England, this denomination stands as the largest in Canada. Evangelical groups have grown and established increased identity in recent years.

Church Unity

If the nineteenth century was one of church division, the

twentieth has been a period of attempted unity. American churchmen have sought to find bases for common action and cooperation, culminating in the 1950 establishment of the National Council of Churches. The international organization known as the World Council of Churches had been founded in 1948.

Pope John XXIII, in 1962, called into session the Second Vatican Council, which sought a "new openness to the world." The resulting change of mood within Roman Catholicism is perhaps the most significant feature in recent Catholic history. The church has not only been moved to greater cooperation with others, but has also been torn by liberal teaching, and nurtured by increased biblical exposure.

Protestant evangelicals have generally not felt at home in the "Council" approach to unity. Weak or liberal theology and questionable social and political practices have led most evangelicals to remain apart from this aspect of the ecumenical movement. However, in 1941, Carl McIntyre led in the establishment of the American Council of Churches which has since become a gravitating point for separatistic, "fundamentalistic" unity. In 1942 the National Association of Evangelicals was founded, giving evangelicals an organization of cooperation which has grown in acceptance and importance.

Para-church organizations have served to unify believers across denominational lines. Christian liberal arts colleges and Bible colleges have brought young people together from varying backgrounds. Youth for Christ, Young Life, Campus Crusade for Christ, Navigators, and Inter-Varsity Christian Fellowship have been not only active evangelism and discipleship ministries, but also agencies of evangelical cooperation.

Several denominational mergers have occurred. Through

the years, Lutheran ethnic and tradition divisions have been brought together. The Lutheran Church in America, the American Lutheran Church, and the Lutheran Church, Missouri Synod, have emerged as the largest bodies of that confession. In 1957, reaching across denominational family lines, the Congregational Church merged with the Evangelical and Reformed Church, a body of German background. The new denomination was named the United Church of Christ. Methodists joined with the Evangelical United Brethren, a German-Methodistic group, to form the United Methodist Church. Conservative EUB churches in the northwest remained apart from the merger and formed the Evangelical Church of North America. The northern branch of Presbyterianism united with the Scottish-derived United Presbyterian Church to organize the United Presbyterian Church.

Although both secular society without and theological defection within have provided strong challenges to the North American church bodies, God has continued to work in individual lives. Perhaps the building of His church has been as extensive in recent years as it has ever been throughout history.

13

Building to the Ends of the Earth

Time line   1500   1600   **1700**   **1800**   **1900**   2000

Our Lord's purpose, when He declared that He would build His church even against the gates of hell itself, was that the body of Christ would be an international body. His Great Commission to His followers was to carry the Gospel, even to the ends of the earth. In this chapter, we shall observe the exciting building of the church around the globe.

Europe

From great success in its earlier history, the Christian church has experienced serious setbacks in modern Europe. Liberal theology, particularly from German theological centers, combined with materialism and political opposition to the faith, have contributed to the decline.

In Great Britain, the evangelical wing of the Church of England has remained vigorous in proclaiming the Gospel of Christ through writing, scholarship, and evangelism. In the nineteenth century, a high church revival took place in

Anglicanism. Led by John Henry Newman, the "Oxford Movement" placed stress upon apostolic succession, formal liturgy, the sacraments, and monasticism. The hymns "Lead Kindly Light," "Faith of Our Fathers," and "Crown Him With Many Crowns" came from this movement.

The dissenting churches grew strikingly in the nineteenth century in Britain, gaining strength from the middle classes. Charles Spurgeon, Baptist pastor of the Metropolitan Tabernacle in London, was the best known spokesman of dissenting Christianity in the period. Spurgeon-led organizations reached thousands for Christ. New groups, like the Plymouth Brethren, rejected a paid ministry and gathered in small fellowship groups. John Nelson Darby, of the Plymouth Brethren, was a principal founder of dispensational theology. To reach the neglected lower classes of British cities, William Booth organized the Salvation Army. The Army featured military organization, uniforms, street meetings, and band music.

Continental Protestantism has suffered serious decline in modern history. Only here and there have elements of vitality surfaced. The pietistic "Inner Mission" movement within Lutheranism has been an example. In Norway, the preaching of layman Hans Nielsen Hauge stirred the rural masses to commitment to Christ in spite of the opposition of the state church.

Participation in foreign missionary outreach, following the example of William Carey, has been an evidence of spiritual vigor. Both in Britain and on the continent, Christians organized for worldwide outreach with notable success.

The fortunes of European Roman Catholicism have ebbed and flowed through modern history. Events in France illustrate the variation. In the seventeenth century, the Jansenist movement, led by August Jansen, scientist Blaise Pascal, and mystic poet Madam Guyon, brought a biblical and pietistic impetus to the church. But the movement was crushed by the state. During the French Revolution in the late eighteenth century, the Roman church suffered from its close association with the monarchy and aristocracy. The revolutionary government advanced anti-Catholic programs for the nations. During the early nineteenth century, a Roman revival occurred, in the wake of a Europewide conservative reaction.

The latter nineteenth century also witnessed a highwater mark of Roman dogmatic claims. In 1854 the dogma of the immaculate conception (the belief that Mary was conceived free from original sin) was promulgated. In 1864, the papacy announced the Syllabus of Errors, repudiating modern political and social practices such as the separation of church and state and public schools. In 1870, the dogma of papal infallibility was proclaimed: the belief that the pope, when he speaks "ex-cathedra" on faith and morals, does so without error. The Old Catholic schism broke from the church over papal infallibility to form a separate group.

The modern papacy has endeavored to relate Roman Catholic principles to a complex age. The church has grappled with the Italian state over territory, promoted scholarship, and aided in labor-management disputes.

The Eastern Orthodox churches of eastern Europe suffered severe curtailment by their communist governments. Although the churches have survived, they have done so in great weakness. Evangelical groups, on the other hand, have grown in unprecedented ways in these regions. Russian Baptist and Pentecostal groups have developed remarkable vigor.

So great has been the overall spiritual decline and lethargy in Europe in the twentieth century, that American mission boards have increasingly engaged in evangelism and church planting on that continent. For example, the Christian and Missionary Alliance ministers in Spain, Germany, the Netherlands, France, and Great Britain. Fledgling evangelical congregations have been planted across western Europe by their efforts.

Latin America

From its earliest European settlement, Latin America has known Roman Catholic influence and domination. Often coupled with animism and spiritism, Catholicism has not followed biblical patterns in building the church. The evangelical message was comparatively late to enter. Governments, influenced by the Roman clergy, opposed Protestant missionary work in many Latin countries. In recent years, the challenges of poverty, leftist political pressure, and secularism among the educated have demonstrated more than ever Latin America's need for the Gospel.

But God has built His church there. An agent of the British and Foreign Bible Society, James Thompson, first reached Argentina in 1820. Thompson introduced the Bible and founded schools in Argentina, Chile, Peru, Ecuador, and Colombia in a six-year period. Another early pioneer was Methodist Bishop William Taylor, who founded schools in the 1870s in Bolivia, Chile, and Peru. Taylor played an influential role in missionary work in Africa as well.

In the late nineteenth century, missionary work was stepped up. Plymouth Brethren missionaries were among the first to work in Venezuela, followed by strong Presbyterian, Evangelical Free, and TEAM contingents. The Orinoco River Mission, founded by Van Eddings in

1920, sought to reach the Indian people of the southeast. American Presbyterians were pioneers in Colombia. The Christian and Missionary Alliance entered that land in 1923. Persecution was often the lot of both missionary and Colombian believer in the early years. As late as 1958, the messenger of Christ faced vigorous opposition.

The Gospel Missionary Union, in 1896, was the first missionary organization to enter Ecuador. The C&MA followed the next year, developing works among the Jivaro and Quechua Indians. The martyrdom, in 1956, of five missionaries by the jungle Aucas of eastern Ecuador stirred worldwide Christian attention. Peru has been the site of work done by Methodist, Nazarene, and Assembly of God groups, among others. The C&MA has ministered there since 1926. The Seventh-Day Adventists have gathered a large following in Peru, as they have in Bolivia and Ecuador. Not until after 1900 was permanent missionary work carried out in Bolivia. Canadian Baptists, the Bolivian Indian Mission, and New Tribes Mission have served there. New Tribes, founded by Paul Fleming, required little training of its personnel. Some served amidst great hardship and even martyrdom.

David Trumbull, in 1845, was the first permanent missionary to enter Chile. Presbyterians and Methodists followed. Henry Weiss entered in 1897 and worked among German settlers. He became the first Christian and Missionary Alliance missionary to that land. Methodists began the first permanent work in Argentina. Allen F. Gardiner, founder of the South American Missionary Society, gave his life in starvation in the desolate regions of Patagonia, south Argentina. His example stirred Europe to send others. The C&MA first entered Argentina in 1897, establishing work in the Buenos Aires area. Southern Baptists also planted strong works. In Paraguay, South

American Missionary Society representative Wilfred Grubb, the Mennonites, and the Free Methodists have worked effectively. Uruguay witnessed Methodist and Italian Waldensian missionary service, the latter beginning in 1858.

French Huguenots attempted to colonize in Brazil in 1555, but had to abandon the effort. In 1855, Dr. Robert Kalley began a work there which established Brazilian Congregationalism. Methodists, Presbyterians, and Southern Baptists have also labored in Brazil. The Unevangelized Fields Mission, organized in 1931, has also shown good results.

In Guyana, a large Anglican church exists as do Protestant communities of other denominations. The Moravians have built the church in Surinam. Little strong church planting has occurred in French Guiana, however.

In Central America, the founding of the Central America Mission by Dr. C. I. Scofield in 1890 opened a path for that society to serve in all nations of that region. The Latin American Mission, founded by Harry Strachan in 1921, also has served with distinction. Friends in Guatamala, Moravians in Honduras and Nicaraugua, Assembly of God in El Salvador, and the Foursquare Church in Panama are among the groups working in this part of Latin America.

Mexico has more than 1,000 missionaries serving with over 100 mission boards. Melinda Rankin, an independent, was the first Protestant missionary to that nation, arriving in 1855. American Baptists were the first organization. The Wycliffe Bible Translators have served among Indian tribal people, not only in Mexico, but also in other Latin countries.

In the West Indies, strong churches have been planted in Jamaica and Puerto Rico. The West Indies Mission has labored effectively in Haiti and the Dominican Republic.

Baptist work in Cuba has been curtailed by the Castroite government, but continues.

The last forty years have witnessed dramatic growth of Pentecostal churches in Latin America. For example, in El Salvador, Pentecostals make up about 75 percent of the Protestant population. In Brazil, that church has seen extraordinary growth. Large Assemblies of God, Church of Christ (Pentecostal), and Brazil for Christ denominations—all Pentecostal—have been built. Indigenous Chilean Pentecostal churches, divided into over 100 denominations, comprise 80 percent of the evangelical force of that nation.

In addition to the countries mentioned above, the Christian and Missionary Alliance has work in Brazil, Uruguay, Venezuela, Guatemala, Costa Rica, Dominican Republic, Mexico, and Puerto Rico.

At first, Latin American people seemed difficult to reach with the Gospel. In recent years a breakthrough has occurred in many nations. God's church is being built in the lands to the south. Missions in Latin America is a moving story of evangelism and church planting.

Asia and the Pacific

Asia, with its large land mass and enormous population, is a continent which the church cannot neglect if it is to fulfill its commission. From the earliest days, Christians have tried to reach this region for Christ.

China, the home of almost one-fourth of the world's population, has been the site of vigorous missionary work. Robert Morrison arrived in the Canton area of south China in 1807, the first Protestant missionary pioneer to that vast nation. In spite of great obstacles, Morrison succeeded in translating the Scriptures into Chinese and in opening the door for others. A cynical shipowner asked Morrison, "And so, Mr. Morrison, you really expect to make an impression on the idolatry of the great Chinese Empire?" Morrison's reply was, "No sir, but I expect God will." Morrison was right! Following the signing of the Treaty of Nanking in 1842, Protestant mission boards—Anglican, Congregational, Baptist, and many others—entered China. The China Inland Mission, founded by J. Hudson Taylor, became the largest missionary force. The CIM became a pattern in their fund-raising methods for the "faith" boards which followed. They concentrated on interior China, utilizing Chinese dress styles and life patterns.

By 1907, 100 years after Morrison's arrival, over 3,400 missionaries labored in China. Persecution hindered, such as the anti-foreign Boxer Rebellion, which martyred 189 missionaries, including 36 of the C&MA. A peak year, 1926, witnessed over 8,000 missionaries in China. Slowly, gradually, a church began to take shape, reaching nearly one million who bore the name "Christian" at one time. The communist victory in the civil war of the late 1940s resulted in the banning of western missionaries from China and in the severe persecution of believers. In spite of this, the greatest disaster the church has ever faced in terms of land area and population, recent signs continue to indicate the presence of God's church in China. Many Alliance workers, like other former China missionaries, took up work in Taiwan, Hong Kong, and among other overseas Chinese after China was closed to western Christians.

Japan remained closed to Christian influence until the 1850s, when the first missionaries arrived. They faced a hostile reaction at first, yet one by one, Japanese accepted the claims of Jesus Christ. A number of boards entered the country, including the Christian and Missionary Alliance in 1888. In 1890, TEAM, founded by Fredrik Franson, made

Japan its first mission field. With little agreement in comity arrangements, Japan became the site of Protestant proliferation and division with other 140 societies working there. The largest church is the Kyodan or United Church of Christ. Still the church remains comparatively small in Japan.

Korea, on the other hand, has been the site of the greatest Christian commuity in Asia. Presbyterians and Methodists first planted the Gospel there in 1885 and continue to have the largest churches. A revival in 1907 spurred growth. The South Korean church has become an example to the world of a giving, praying, witnessing body. In North Korea the church has been driven underground by communist control.

Southeast Asia was also reached early by missionary outreach. Adoniram Judson arrived in Burma in 1813. A Baptist church was established, especially strong among the Karen and Kachin tribes people. In spite of a government decree against western missionaries in 1966, the church is growing and progressing. The C&MA was for many years the only Protestant agency in Indo-China. Dr. Robert Jaffrey began work there in 1911 which grew into the strong Evangelical Church of Viet Nam. Laos and Cambodia were less responsive to C&MA efforts, although a church among the Meo or Hmong tribes people in Laos was making considerable progress. The horrors of the wars of the last thirty years have proven disruptive and costly to the church. Its witness, though curtailed, continues in spite of great suffering.

Thailand has allowed missionaries since the 1820s. The Presbyterians planted a major church there; the C&MA arrived in 1929 to work in the northeast part of the country. The Thai have remained generally resistant to the Gospel and loyal to Buddhism. Only a small church exists there today. In Malaysia, Islam has provided the barrier to church growth. The Chinese community in nearby Singapore has been somewhat more responsive.

India, with its teeming population, has been another significant center of Christian missionary work. The Danish-Halle team of Ziegenbalg and Plutschau, and the intrepid William Carey have already been noted in chapter nine as pioneers in India. Both European and American mission boards established churches in the years following. Congregationalists planted a church in south India, Presbyterians in north. Baptists centered their work in Nagaland in northeast India, there to experience the greatest successes and to build a strong church. The Christian and Missionary Alliance began work in east-central India in 1887. In recent years, Pentecostalism has spread in some parts of that land. Much remains to be done; yet God's church is being built in India.

Sri Lanka, or Ceylon, has been the site of missionary work since 1804. A fairly strong Roman Catholic church exists on the island. The Anglicans are the largest Protestant group. No Christian organization, however, has made a strong impact on this Buddhist nation. Nepal, completely closed to the Gospel until a revolution in 1950, has opened its door a crack to allow secular-aid project ministries. Prem Pradham has given the minuscule Nepalese Christian community strong national leadership. Pakistan, with its dominantly Muslim population, has been served by Presbyterians, World Wide Evangelization Crusade, TEAM, and Conservative Baptists. A church is emerging. Bangladesh, one of the most poverty-stricken and neglected areas of the world, has a Baptist witness, among others.

The Philippines became strongly Roman Catholic in the many decades Spain occupied the territory. Protestantism has grown since American occupation in the 1890s. Numerous mission boards, including the C&MA in 1902, have entered the country. The United Church of the Philippines, a merger of five denominations, is the largest church. The Christian and Missionary Alliance in the Philippines is a thriving national church and one of the fastest growing in the world. Far Eastern Gospel Crusade, beginning with a team of ex-American soldiers who had served there in World War II, and Far Eastern Broadcasting Company are among the more recent missionary groups working there.

Dutch Reformed chaplains and pastors planted the first and largest Protestant churches in Indonesia. The Batak Church of Sumatra is another large group in that land. The Christian and Missionary Alliance work in Kalimantan, opened in 1929, has been one of the most fruitful areas on earth with thousands of Dyack people active in a vibrant church. The exciting story of the beginnings of missionary work among Stone Age people in Irian Jaya has culminated in another growing church.

Across Oceania, the church has been built. Anglicans in the Solomons and New Hebrides, Methodists on Tonga and the Fijis, Congregationalists in Samoa and the Marshall Islands, and Lutherans on Papua-New Guinea have all played their parts. A plaque in memory of Scottish Presbyterian John Geddie reading, "When he landed in 1848 there were no Christians here; when he left in 1872, there were no heathen," typifies the advance of the Gospel in this area. Australia and New Zealand have joined hands with the North American churches in the support of world evangelism. The Alliance began ministry in these countries in the early 1970s.

Southwest Asia and the Near East

In the Muslim Near East, however, the building of the church has been very difficult. Afghanistan has only recently allowed Dr. J. Christy Wilson to found churches, for foreigners only. Iran enjoyed the benefit of a Persian Bible translation by pioneer Henry Martyn early in the nineteenth century and of Operation Mobilization efforts. The nation has recently returned to a strongly Islamic state. Iraq allows no American missionaries; Christians are few. Turkey may have 10,000 Protestants. Lebanon has a sizeable population of Maronite Christians and has experienced significant educational work done by Presbyterians. Syria, however, has no missionaries and a very small evangelical community. In Jordan, a tiny Anglican community exists. The states of the Arabian peninsula have been very reluctant to allow any penetration of the Gospel. Samuel Zwemer endeavored for sixty years to reach this area for Christ. He gained a reputation as an "Apostle to the Muslims." Israel, a Jewish island in an Islamic sea, has remained equally resistant to evangelical missions. While a small church exists in the Near East, its construction has been exceedingly slow and small. The Christian and Missionary Alliance ministers in Israel, Lebanon, Jordon and Syria.

Africa

Missionary work began in Africa in the late eighteenth century. However, two famous pioneers of the early nineteenth century brought worldwide attention to that continent. Robert Moffat began his fifty-three-year career in South Africa in 1817. Sent by the London Missionary Society, Moffat initiated Gospel work among the Bechuana tribe. David Livingstone arrived in South Africa in 1840 to engage in missionary work, vigorous exploration, and concern for the evils of the slave trade. Livingstone's work, publicized by the newsman Henry Stanley, caused Christians to respond to the missionary cause, forming missionary organizations to promote the Gospel on the continent of Africa.

South Africa, Malawi, Zambia, Tanzania, and Zaire—all were touched by servants of Christ sent under the aegis of Livingstone-inspired missionary groups. In South Africa, the European settlers who dominate the nation, give their allegiance to the Dutch Reformed and Anglican churches. In addition, the Black population has been reached by Moravian, Methodist, The Evangelical Alliance Mission (TEAM), and other missionary groups. The Christian population of South Africa is among the highest on the continent. Zambia also has a strong Christian community. Perhaps 70 percent of the nation professes to be Christian. The United Church of Zambia, a merger of six denominations, is the largest church. The Africa Evangelical Fellowship and the Plymouth Brethren also have strong groups in Zambia.

The Protestant community in Zaire numbers more than two million. The C&MA sent its first missionaries there in 1884, amidst great hardship. The first thirty years saw thirty missionary graves. Evangelical Free, Covenant, Kimbangu separatist church, and many others are a part of the Christian community. Southwest Africa, Lesotho, and Swaziland also have growing churches. In Angola and Mozambique, Roman Catholicism, from the long period of Portuguese control, is a large force. Intrepid Methodist Bishop Taylor began works in both these countries. In Zimbabwe-Rhodesia, Anglican and Methodist churches are large and influential. Methodist Bishop Muzorewa is a strong political figure in the country.

In east Africa, substantial progress has been made. Although Roman Catholicism is strong in little Rwanda and Burundi dating from Belgian control, a Protestant witness is growing in both countries. Lutheran churches have developed strongly in Tanzania, where Moravians, Pentecostals, and Mennonites have also labored with success. The Anglican church comprises over 90 percent of the Protestants in Uganda. Their Bishop Festo Kivengere has gained a hearing in the worldwide evangelical community. Kenya was the scene of the establishment of the Africa Inland Mission, founded in 1898 by Peter Scott. A strong church has been planted there. Ethiopia's Ethiopian Orthodox church is descended from ancient Coptic roots and has had an important role in the political history of the country. Sudan Interior Mission, Presbyterian, and Baptist General Conference forces have labored there. The expulsion of many missionary personnel after the revolution in the 1970s, has created uncertainty and turmoil for the church there. Somalia is almost solidly Muslim. Very few have been won to Christ by missionary effort.

West Africa was the scene of great hardship and loss of life for missionary personnel in the early days. An unfavorable climate took a high toll. The burgeoning church there is a monument to the sacrifice of early pioneers. In Sierra Leone, a British colony for freed slaves, Baptists, Methodists, Evangelical United Brethren, C&MA, and other missionaries planted the Gospel. In Liberia, an outpost for freed American slaves. Black missionaries Lott Carey and Colin Teague were effective early pioneers. American black missionary societies, the Lott Carey Baptist Society and the National Baptist Convention, continued the work. Radio station ELWA has had a powerful ministry.

Islam has retarded the growth of the church in Senegal, Gambia, Guinea, Mali, and Niger, although missionary work has been carried on in each. The Christian and Missionary Alliance has been active in Guinea since 1918 and Mali since 1923. In the Ivory Coast an exciting mass movement led by the legendary Prophet Harris in 1913 won thousands to Christ. Methodists, C&MA, Conservative Baptists, and Southern Baptists have served there more recently, building a strong church. Upper Volta and Togo have Roman Catholic churches of some numbers, based upon the French period of their history. The Assembly of God in Upper Volta and a German mission in Togo were the first Protestant witnesses. Black Christians from Jamaica helped build the church in Ghana; English Methodists did so in Dahomey. Baptists have served effectively in Cameroon, Central African Empire, and Chad. The Christian and Missionary Alliance has established work in Upper Volta and Gabon. The church in these lands has enjoyed unprecedented growth over the last decade.

Perhaps the strongest church in West Africa exists in Nigeria. The Southern Baptists began work there in 1850, the first of their seventy-one mission fields. They have expanded into several neighboring nations as well. Scottish Presbyterians, including the famous Mary Slessor of Calabar, ministered there. The Sudan Interior Mission, founded by Rowland Bingham in 1901, has almost half the Protestant missionaries in Nigeria, an effective periodical *Africa Challenge,* and a strong church, the Evangelical Church of West Africa. SIM ministers also in other African countries.

The story of the building of the church in North Africa not been as encouraging. Islam has proved resistant to the Gospel. Libya has had no missionaries since 1957 and has few, if any, national Christians. Algeria was the site of the founding of the North Africa Mission in 1881. That board served there, in Tunisia, and in Morocco. In Egypt the ancient Coptic church has experienced some renewal recently with increased emphasis upon Bible reading. Anglican, Presbyterian, Free Methodist, and Church of God (Cleveland, Tennessee) groups have founded Protestant churches. In the Sudan, the Islamic north has been slow to respond. The Black and animist south has been more open to the Gospel.

Africa has been a continent of great church growth in the last decade. Not only missionary-related churches, but independent indigenous movements have greatly increased the work of Christ. Experts have predicted that if present growth rates continue, Africa may become the most Christian of all continents in the future.

The building of God's church has extended around the globe. The Great Commission has been faithfully carried out by men and women of many nations and denominations. While much yet remains to be done, it is thrilling to see the fulfillment of Jesus' promise that He would build His church.

Epilogue

Almost two thousand years have passed since Jesus uttered those telling words, "I will build my church." The years since are witnesses to the absolute faithfulness of God's promise and the continuing progress of Christ's church.

Christianity spread throughout the Roman world, capturing the hearts of men and women in spite of travel difficulties and governmental persecution. A strong witness was established with vigorous leadership, thoughtful writing, and profound theology. When man-made religious inventions threatened the truth in the Middle Ages, the light of the Gospel was kept burning by faithful monks, mystics, and separatists. The Reformation saw Luther, Zwingli, Calvin, the Anabaptists, and others place emphasis again upon the Bible and salvation by faith. God used renewal movements like the Puritans, Wesleyans, Pietists, Moravians, and Jansenists to reinvigorate the building process. America, with its wide liberty, became a great center of church life and activity. Even though some segments of European Christianity waned, the message of the good news found acceptance in other lands. Brazil, Korea, and parts of Africa established vigorous churches.

The twentieth century church faces a world beset by severe problems. Burgeoning population means food shortages and starvation. Poverty and want are the lot of millions. Unemployment, inflation, and energy crises plague industrialized nations. Racism and injustice permeate the globe. An atheistic communism and a resurgent Islam threaten the Christian message. Many of the world's peoples—from Japan and France to the intellectuals of Latin America—have abandoned religion and are avowedly secularists. War breaks out frequently. Materialism rears its head everywhere.

The Christian might be tempted to look at such an environment in complete despair. "How can anything be done in a world beset by such trouble?" he is apt to ask.

The message of church history echoes back to just such a question. Yes, something can be done in the face of mounting difficulty! God is not limited by circumstances. He has brought men and women to Himself, nurtured them in the faith, guided them in their daily walk. What He has done before, He can and will do again. The church is not dead nor is it irrelevant—it is God's institution, Christ's very body.

Great progress in the spread of the Gospel is occurring in our age. More men and women are responding to Christ in Africa and Latin America than ever before. The church in North America exhibits continuing signs of life. Cracks are beginning to appear in the strong opposition to Christianity which has existed so long in China. Opportunities for evangelism abound around the world. The doubting and discouraged believer finds new reason for confidence and more complete trust. Although the very gates of hell itself rage, they cannot prevail. God has built, is building, and will continue to build His church on Christ the Cornerstone.

GLOSSARY OF TERMS

Achaia   modern southern Greece.

Allegorize   to read hidden or mystic meaning into the Scriptures.

Americanist heresy   supposed heresy of nineteenth century American Catholics overemphasizing assimilation into American culture to the neglect of loyalty to Catholicism.

Anabaptist   "rebaptizer," term of derision given those of the sixteenth century who, denying infant baptism, practiced believers' baptism.

Anglican   or Church of England; sixteenth century reformation group.

Annate   a tax of the first year's income of an appointee to church office.

Annulment an invalidating of a marriage as never legally correct.

Apologists writers of early church who defended the faith against antagonists.

Arianism a heresy of the fourth century, after Arius its founder, which believed Jesus to be the highest of created beings, not God.

Armenia the kingdom whose monarch became the first Christian king, located on the Turkish-Iranian-U.S.S.R. border today.

Arminian the beliefs or followers of Arminius; emphasizing man's role in the salvation experience.

Ascetic given to strict self-denial, for the sake of spiritual benefit.

Asia Minor modern Turkey; prominent location of early church strength.

Augsburg Confession principal Lutheran doctrinal statement of the reformation, written by Philip Melancthon.

Augustinian a monastic order, named for the fifth century church leader, emphasizing preaching and personal piety, to which Luther belonged.

Ban ouster or excommunication from the church for flagrant sin, heresy, or schism, as practiced by the Mennonites.

Baptistic pertaining to the belief in and practice of believers' baptism as opposed to infant baptism.

Barbarians Germanic invaders of the Roman Empire from the fourth through the seventh centuries.

Bishop church leader; in the early church the central figure of believers in a city; from the Middle Ages on, the head of a diocese or group of churches.

Boxer Rebellion insurrection in China, 1899ff, which resulted in the deaths of several missionaries.

Brethren of the Common Life fifteenth century German and Dutch association to promote education and piety.

Byzantine the empire and culture centering in Constantinople during medieval times.

Canton a Swiss province.

Cardinal a churchman, appointed by the pope, who is a member of the college of cardinals, an advisory body and the group which elects popes.

Cathari twelfth century heresy, widespread in southern France and northern Italy, dualistic in belief.

Cathedral a church which contains a bishop's seat or headquarters, usually a large, important church.

Celibacy the state of being unmarried, as monks under a vow not to marry.

Cistercians the monastic order, founded at Citeaux, France, in 1098, very strict, influential.

Comity a policy whereby mission boards agree to divide territory to avoid duplication and competition.

Communalism the practice of owning land and goods in common; practiced in the early church, in medieval monasticism, and in nineteenth century America.

Conciliar movement an attempt in the fourteenth and fifteenth centuries to broaden the church's authority base, to councils representative of the whole church.

Congregational the policy that church governing authority rests solely with the local congregation; a denomination holding that view.

Consubstantiation the Lutheran belief that the presence of Christ exists in, with, and under the elements of communion.

Creed a brief formula of doctrinal belief.

Crusade one of the military expeditions of the eleventh century and following, to rescue the Holy Land from the Muslims.

Deism belief in a god who created the world, but remains beyond the range of human experience.

Depravity the belief that man is innately sinful.

Didache or **Teaching** a second century explanation of how church life should be carried out; an important source of information on the early church.

Dissenter one who dissents from an established state church, as English Protestants not conforming to the Church of England.

Dispensationalism a system of doctrine after nineteenth century British origins, closely dividing the eras of Divine-human contact.

Dominicans a monastic order founded by Dominic in the twelfth century; significant in education and scholarship.

Donation of Constantine a document giving the papacy temporal authority in the west and primacy over other churchmen; proven a forgery in the Renaissance.

Donatism rigorist separatistic movement of the fourth and fifth centuries.

Ebionism an attempt to combine Judaism and Christianity in the second century; resulted in heretical doctrine, denying the deity of Christ.

Ecumenical pertaining to church unity or cooperation efforts, often applied to non-evangelical attempts in this direction.

Election the doctrine of Divine choice; predestining of individuals as objects of salvation.

Enlightenment eighteenth century philosophic movement characterized by questioning of authority, political theorizing, empirical science, and anti-Christian polemic.

Establishment a church organization having legal, government recognition and support, such as the Church of England and Lutheran bodies in Scandinavia.

Excommunicate to cut off from the church.

Extreme unction the sacrament given by a Roman Catholic priest to one in danger of death.

Faith mission a missionary organization which is independent of denominational control, and which guarantees no fixed salary.

Feudalism a system of land tenure in return for military service; broadened, in the medieval era, to include other socio-economic relationships.

Franciscans a monastic order founded by Francis of Assisi in the twelfth century, emphasizing ministry to the poor.

Friar a member of a religious order, especially one of the mendicant or begging orders.

Fundamentalist one upholding fundamental doctrinal positions, as opposed to liberal theology or practice; late nineteenth and early twentieth century America; more recently, an advocate of separatistic, combative orthodox Protestantism.

Gathered church   a concept of the church stressing voluntary association of believers, as opposed to state church inclusivism.

Gnosticism   a religious belief of the second century and following having several forms, some with Christian terminology; dualistic, stressing salvation by gnosis, or knowledge.

Great Schism   the schism in the church, 1378-1415, where Europe divides between popes reigning in Rome and Avignon, France.

Holy Roman Empire   a political entity of the Middle Ages and early modern times encompassing modern Germany.

Huguenot   a French Calvinist Protestant.

Humanism   the study of humanities through the revival of the Greek and Roman classics in the Renaissance era. In Italy, tending toward secularistic emphases, in northern Europe more religious.

Icon   a picture used for religious expression; the subject of controversy in the eastern church.

Immaculate Conception   Roman Catholic dogma, proclaimed in 1854, that Mary was conceived free from original sin.

Independents   English Puritan movement of the seventeenth century holding to congregational church government in a state church.

Index a list of books prohibited by the Roman Catholic church.

Indulgence Roman Catholic system of remission of the temporal or purgatorial penalties for sin.

Inquisition a systematic pursuit of heresy and its punishment.

Investiture a medieval controversy between church and secular authorities over the selection of high church officials.

Interdict the prohibiting of the dispensing of the sacraments across a given area.

Islam the religion of one god, Allah, and Mohammed, his prophet.

Jansenism a seventeenth century French movement within Roman Catholicism, stressing predestination, grace, and personal piety.

Jesuits a monastic order, founded in the sixteenth century by Ignatius Loyola, active in the Catholic Reformation.

Justification the doctrine of man's being made acceptable to God.

Koine the common Greek dialect used in the writing of the New Testament.

Macedonia the district around Philippi in Roman times; today northern Greece and southern Yugoslavia.

Manichaeism a system of belief founded by Mani in the third century, combining Zoroastrianism, Christianity, and other ideas.

Mar Thoma an early Christian community in India, traditionally thought founded by the apostle Thomas.

Medieval pertaining to the Middle Ages, roughly from 500 to 1500.

Mendicant living by alms, begging, as the Franciscan and Dominican monastic orders.

Mennonite a Reformation group, derived from the Anabaptists, named after Mennon Simons, characterized by believers' baptism and the separation of church and state.

Modernist one who follows modern, critical methods of biblical study, one who denies the authority of Scripture or other orthodox Protestant beliefs; United States, late nineteenth and early twentieth centuries.

Monarchianism a heretical tendency in the early church denying the trinity.

Monophysites an early heresy holding that there is but a single nature in Christ.

Montanism a schismatic group of the early church stressing strictness of life, the Spirit's continued revelation.

Moravianism a Protestant renewal group, based on early Hussite origins, reconstituted in the 1720s, stressing foreign missions.

Mystics, German late fourteenth and early fifteenth century Christians who emphasized the experience of the Christian life, personal communion with God.

Nation state a unified government and territory composed of people of like customs, language, forming in the High Middle Ages in western Europe.

Neo-orthodoxy a twentieth century emphasis in theology, after Karl Barth and Emil Brunner, protesting Protestant liberal theology's confidence in man.

Neo-Platonism a philosophy of the early church era, ascetic, pantheistic, influential upon the church.

Novatianism a rigorist, schismatic group of the early church.

Oxford Movement a nineteenth century movement within the Church of England stressing apostolic succession and the sacraments.

Papal infallibility dogma promulgated in Roman Catholicism in 1870 that the pope, when he speaks officially on faith and morals, cannot err.

Pax Romana Roman peace; the period of the New Testament of relative civil tranquility.

Peasants' Revolt a sixteenth century uprising of the lower classes, using some of Luther's ideas as rationale.

Penance a Roman Catholic sacrament consisting of repentance, confession to a priest, satisfaction, and absolution.

Pentecostal twentieth century movement holding to speaking in tongues as the evidence of the filling of the Holy Spirit.

Perfection John Wesley's view of sanctification whereby the believer is made perfect in love.

Pietism a seventeenth century German Lutheran movement emphasizing personal Christian experience, Bible study, and prayer.

Polemicists early church writers who attacked heresy and other error within the church.

Post-apostolic the period after the close of the New Testament, basically the second and third centuries.

Presbyterian a system of church government utilizing the representative system; the state church of Scotland; an American denomination of Calvinistic descent.

Protestatio a statement of faith issued by Lutheran leadership in the Reformation era.

Protracted meetings a series of evangelistic meetings popularized by Charles Finney in nineteenth century America.

Puritan in sixteenth and seventeenth century England, one who desired to purify the Anglican Church of its Roman Catholic vestiges; immigrants to America of similar persuasion.

Reformation the sixteenth century renewal movement, led by Luther, Zwingli, Calvin, and others, which resulted in Protestantism.

Reformed those Protestant churches founded by Zwingli, and Calvin and their descendants.

Relics objects venerated because of association with a saint.

Remonstrants followers of James Arminius in the seventeenth century in the Netherlands who opposed strict Calvinism.

Renaissance the rebirth of classical learning and culture in the transition era between medieval and modern history.

Sacrament A rite of the church, often understood to convey grace, as in the seven Roman Catholic sacraments: baptism, the Eucharist, confirmation, penance, extreme unction, ordination, and matrimony.

Sanctification the doctrine of being set apart unto God, having one's life made more godly.

Scala Sancta the sacred staircase in Rome, supposedly used in Pilate's judgment hall at the time of Christ, which Luther venerated during his 1510 visit.

Glossary 173

Scholasticism the dominant Christian philosophy of the Middle Ages wherein Christian doctrine was expressed in Aristotalian forms.

Separatists Those who depart from an established church; particularly Englishmen of the seventeenth century who espoused separated congregational forms.

Shakers a heretical religious communal sect of the American frontier.

Slavic a group of people related in language and cultural forms who inhabit eastern Europe: Russians, Czechs, Poles, etc.

Sovereignty the doctrine that God is supreme in wisdom, power, and authority.

Territorial church system of organization in Germany in the post-Reformation era whereby the separate provinces determined whether the church would be Protestant or Catholic.

Thirty-Nine Articles Anglican doctrinal statement of the Reformation period.

Tory a person in America favoring retaining ties with Great Britain in the Revolutionary War era.

Transubstantiation the belief that the bread and wine of communion become, to the eye of faith, the body and blood of Christ, when duly consecrated by a priest.

TULIP a mnemonic device used to highlight five points of

John Calvin's theology.

Unitarian   one who denies the doctrine of the trinity, who believes God exists in only one person; a denomination holding that belief.

Universalism   the doctrine that all men eventually will be saved.

Voluntarism   the practice of voluntary association of Christians in self-supporting churches as opposed to the state church concept.

Waldensians   a sect of dissenters from the Roman church in the twelfth century who stressed simplicity of life and Bible reading.

Westminster Confession   a doctrinal statement, framed in seventeenth century England, expressing Presbyterian belief.

BIBLIOGRAPHY

I. GENERAL WORKS

Baillie, John, editor, *Library of Christian Classics*, 26 vols., Westminster Press.
Cairnes, Earle, *Christianity Through the Centuries*, Zondervan.
Dowley, Tim, editor, *Handbook to the History of Christianity*, Wm. B. Eerdmans.
Latourette, Kenneth, *Christianity Through the Ages*, Harper.
Latourette, Kenneth, *A History of Christianity*, Harper.
Schaff, Philip, *History of the Christian Church*, 8 vols., Eerdmans.
Walker, Williston, *A History of the Christian Church*, Charles Scribner's Sons.

II. THE ANCIENT CHURCH, chapters 1-3.

Augustine, *Confessions*, Thomas Nelson and Sons.
Bonner, Gerald, *St. Augustine of Hippo*, Westminster.

Bruce, F. F., *The Spreading Flame*, Eerdmans.
Grant, Robert, *Augustine to Constantine*, Harper and Row.
Grant, Robert, *Early Christianity and Society*, Harper and Row.
Roberts, Alexander and James Donaldson, editors, *The Ante-Nicene Fathers*, 10 vols., Eerdmans.
Schaff, Philip and Henry Wace, editors, *The Nicene and Post-Nicene Fathers*, 14 vols., Eerdmans.
Yamauchi, Edwin, "How the Early Church Responded to Social Problems," *Christianity Today*, November 24, 1972.

III. THE MEDIEVAL CHURCH, chapters 4-5.

Bainton, Roland, *Early and Medieval Christianity*, Beacon Press.
Bedoyere, Michael de la, *Francis, A Biography of the Saint of Assisi*, Harper and Row.
Cannon, William, *History of Christianity in the Middle Ages*, Abingdon.
Hoyt, Robert, *Europe in the Middle Ages*, Harcourt, Brace, and World.
Kempis, Thomas a', *The Imitation of Christ*, Harper and Brothers.
Parker, G. H. W., *The Morning Star*, Eerdmans.
Walker, G. S. M., *The Growing Storm*, Eerdmans.

IV. THE REFORMATION, chapters 6-7.

Bainton, Roland, *Here I Stand, A Life of Martin Luther*, Abingdon.
Bainton, Roland, *The Reformation of the Sixteenth Century*, Beacon Press.

Clason, Claus, *Anabaptism; a Social History*, Cornell University.
Hillerbrand, Hans, *The Reformation*, Harper and Row.
Lucas, Henry, *Renaissance and the Reformation*, Harper and Row.
Parker, T. H., *Portrait of Calvin*, Westminster.
Parker, T. M., *The English Reformation to 1558*, Oxford.
Potter, G. R., *Zwingli*, Cambridge University Press.

V. CATHOLIC REFORMATION, POST-REFORMATION, AGE OF REVIVAL, chapters 8-9.

Bangs, Carl, *Arminius*, Abingdon.
Bunyan, John, *Pilgrim's Progress*, Fleming Revell.
Knappen, M. N., *Tudor Puritanism*, Peter Smith.
McConnell, Francis, *John Wesley*, Abingdon.
Olin, John C., *The Catholic Reformation: Savonarola to Ignatius Loyola*, Harper and Row.
Thompson, James, *The Wars of Religion in France*, Ungar.
Weinlick, John, *Count Zinzendorf*, Abingdon.
Wood, A. Skevington, *The Inextinguishable Blaze*, Eerdmans.

VI. THE AMERICAN CHURCH, chapters 10-12.

Cartwright, Peter, *Autobiography*, Abingdon.
Ellis, John Tracy, *American Catholicism*, University of Chicago.
Finney, Charles, *Memoirs*, A. S. Barnes.
Gaustad, Edwin, *A Religious History of America*, Harper and Row.
Hudson, Winthrop, *Religion in America*, Scribners.
Poling, David, *Why Billy Graham?* Zondervan.
Sweet, William, *Religion in Colonial America*, Scribners.

Sweet, William, *Religion on the American Frontier*, 4 vols., Cooper Square.

Tozer, A. W., *Wingspread*, Christian Publications, Inc.

Winslow, Ola, *Jonathan Edwards*, Octagon.

VII. TO THE ENDS OF THE EARTH, chapter 13.

Alliance Witness, The, August 22, 1979.

Anderson, Courtney, *To the Golden Shore, The Life of Adoniram Judson*, Little Brown and Co.

Blaikie, W. Garden, *The Life of David Livingstone*, Fleming H. Revell.

Detzler, Wayne, *The Changing Church in Europe*, Zondervan.

Kane, J. Herbert, *A Concise History of the Christian World Mission*, Baker.

Kane, J. Herbert, *A Global View of World Missions*, Baker.

Latourette, Kenneth, *A History of the Expansion of Christianity*, 7 vols., Zondervan.

Thiessen, John, *A Survey of World Missions*, Inter-Varsity Press.